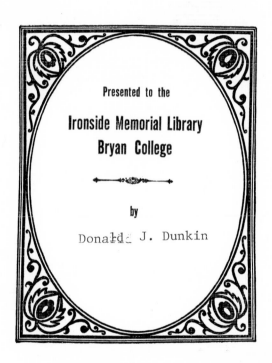

Presented to the

Ironside Memorial Library
Bryan College

by

Donald J. Dunkin

Harvest
of Yesterdays

Gladys Taber

Harvest
of Yesterdays ❧

Drawings by Pamela Johnson

J. B. LIPPINCOTT COMPANY
Philadelphia and New York

U.S. Library of Congress Cataloging in Publication Data

Taber, Gladys Bagg, birth date
    Harvest of yesterdays.
    Autobiographical.
    1. Taber, Gladys Bagg, birth date—Biography.
I. Title.
PS3539.A136Z52   818'.5'209 [B]   75–44003
ISBN–0–397–01133–4

By Gladys Taber

HARVEST OF YESTERDAYS

COUNTRY CHRONICLE

MY OWN COOK BOOK
From Stillmeadow and Cape Cod

MY OWN CAPE COD

AMBER, A VERY PERSONAL CAT

STILLMEADOW ALBUM

STILLMEADOW CALENDAR
A Countrywoman's Journal

GLADYS TABER'S STILLMEADOW COOK BOOK

ANOTHER PATH

THE STILLMEADOW ROAD

STILLMEADOW SAMPLER

STILLMEADOW DAYBOOK

TO
Charles Schlessiger
WITH LOVE AND APPRECIATION FOR
HIS WISDOM, PATIENCE AND ENCOURAGEMENT
THROUGH SO MANY HARVESTS
IN MY LITERARY FIELD

Contents

Harvest
of Yesterdays

Preface

I usually skip prefaces when I read a book. I feel that a book should explain itself by the contents. When I eat a ripe rosy apple, I skip peeling and begin crunching.

But there can be exceptions and in some cases a preface is like a gate opening to the inner domain. If it makes a reader feel at home, it is desirable. So—here is a preface.

It is easier to say what this book is not than what it is. It is not a true memoir nor an autobiography, but it is a collection of memories of people, places and animals and the impact of the particular time I happened to be born in.

The history of this time I must leave to the experts, partly because I am completely unable to remember any dates except the Battle of Hastings in 1066 and unfortunately do not recall what it was all about. However, I remember vividly that I was wrapping Christmas presents when the news of Pearl Harbor came over the desk radio. Consequently the horror of Pearl Harbor brings back to me the sound of gay Christmas wrappings falling on the floor as I sat with my head in my hands and wept.

I think of my memories as tucked away in an ebony treasure box like rough-cut jewels, often with no settings, just colored stones, some midnight black, some golden as sunrise over the sea, some the peaceful hue of chalcedony. When I hold one in my hand, chosen at random, I live completely in the spell it casts.

Because I have written over fifty books and countless personal columns, my reader-friends have shared a good deal already with me, especially in the Stillmeadow books based on my daily journals of country living. But the happenings I write about now, as well as my feelings and thoughts, are those that persist in my heart today, this hour, this minute, and I have tried to assemble them as if I were stringing those rough-cut stones on a single strand.

Then they may go back in the ebony box as I face the adventures of tomorrow.

Travelin' Man

I AM THINKING about the past today for I have been reading Alistair Cooke's *America*. I always wanted to study history but when I went to college one took the prescribed courses and did not argue. As an English major, all I could manage was one course in History of the Reformation. Certainly one course could not make me understand that complicated period.

But I wonder whether we can ever understand the past, for we cannot have complete empathy with it since we live in the present. I suspect this is also true of our own personal past. It has to be colored by the experience of living today.

We add to it or subtract from it. We are products of it, to be sure, but we cannot relive it with immediacy. This is why I distrust memoirs.

What most memoirs do for me, however, is to illuminate the personality of the writer, for this always comes through. Yesterday may have influenced our tomorrow but we are still individual. What we feel and think is our own possession. But the business of living is sharing, so I always want to know all about everything that has happened to people I care for. Then I feel a small door has been opened and perhaps I may step inside briefly and be less lonely.

It is tempting to believe others care about that first blinding of love or that first unbearable sorrow. Usually they don't. They are islanded in their own memories. But occasionally someone says, "Oh, do tell me where you were born!"

And being born is a beginning. Even if one believes in reincarnation, it is the beginning of one lifetime on this particular planet in this era.

I was born in the wrong place. I was born in Colorado, which may well be one of the loveliest states in the union. But the New England relatives were shocked. They felt my mother and father ought at least to have managed to come back to Massachusetts so I would be born where most of the ancestors had been. It was almost as if I were illegal.

What compounded the error was that my older sister, Majel, and my younger brother, Walter, also were aliens. Neither of them was born in New England and both died in infancy of what was then called cholera morbus. The grandparents felt sure that in Massachusetts they would have flourished! Instead, they were buried there, brought cross country by train to the family cemetery in West Springfield. As the only survivor, many times in my childhood I felt apologetic. I thought my bones too should be with theirs back in New England.

My father's family, named Bagg, were descendants of Richard and Cotton Mather. They came from England in time to help found colleges and build churches. Cotton was more colorful for he was involved in the witch burning, although he did a good deal in other more useful areas. Richard first became famous when the ship coming from England was about to founder in a hurricane and he donned his ministerial robes and spoke to God, as God presumably watched him clinging to the mast. The ship did not sink and the passengers laid it to Richard's influence with God.

On my mother's side were the Hatches and Raybolds, who came a bit later. One of the Hatches is buried in Boston in the ancient cemetery by Trinity Church. The men all seem to have been ministers and educators. Another Hatch, Leonidas, served in the Civil War and died of what they called consumption. I inherited my middle name from him, the feminine version Leonae. He was spoken of as "poor Uncle Lonnie." I used to look at the daguerreotype of him in his curious uniform and wonder about his time in the war.

I do not know much about any of the Raybolds except Uncle Walter and Grandmother Raybold. The truth is the Bagg family (the Mather descendants) were so colorful and dominating that they seemed to me like royalty and outshone all the other relatives.

I grew up looking at a heavy volume of the Mather genealogy and mainly noticing how much all the gentlemen in the engravings resembled my father. I read a bit here and there and noted one reverend who left to his wife, Sarah, mother of his nine children, just half of his house when he died; the other half belonged to the oldest son. It was a man's world then, and as far as my father was concerned it always would be. I also read about Cotton Mather being such a dedicated father that he took his four-and-a-half-year-old daughter in his lap and described hell to her until she "had a fit."

As I think about these early people, I wonder what gave them the courage to come to a wilderness land across a dark, stormy ocean. They had broken with the Church of England, it is true, but I also think they had a dream of a new world made to their specifications. And a longing for adventure must have been there along with the vision. They left comfortable homes in English villages and towns and secure positions as ministers of God. And they dragged their wives with them, willing or not.

Rufus Mather Bagg, my grandfather, was happy to settle in Riverdale, Massachusetts, on a stretch of rich farmland by the river. His brother Aaron settled there, too, in a huge pink stone house. Grandfather's house was a stately mansion with pillars, countless rooms and frescoed ceilings. I remember the painted cupids cavorting overhead in the parlor. There was room enough in the big dining room for the eight children and guests. The kitchen was as big as most living rooms of today and an Irish cook presided over the huge cast-iron range.

Outside were the barns, silos, icehouse, chicken houses, pigpens and storage buildings. The farm crew came from the neighboring area. The household help lived in, on the third floor.

As his sons grew up, Grandfather gave them houses. Uncle Ed lived across the road, and Uncle Fred next door. Uncle Lisha eventually moved out of the enclave to Wollaston. The girls went as far away as the New England Conservatory of Music and three of them married and lived in

Massachusetts as they should. Aunt Laura, the eldest, eloped to Colorado with an amiable gentleman who was a beekeeper and this was probably Grandfather's greatest grief.

Or it was until Rufus Mather Bagg, Jr., my father, the eldest son, decided he did not want to settle down. He must have inherited some of the blood of those early men who left England to seek a far horizon. He began, quite reasonably, by going to Amherst but then went off to Johns Hopkins. It seemed as far away as Africa would nowadays. There he got his Ph.D., took a position as geology instructor and was engaged in the geological survey of Maryland.

On looking back I can see he would never have made a successful farmer. When I was very small I used to see him out in his vegetable patch, digging things up to see why they weren't growing faster. Mama used to suggest that if he left them alone they might make it.

My mother came into his life when he came home for the holidays. Uncle Ed was courting her and introduced them. After one meeting my father told Ed he had to stop seeing Grace Raybold because she was going to be his own. Few people ever crossed Papa successfully and Uncle Ed was not one of them.

The wedding ceremony was performed by the bride's grandfather, the Reverend W. H. Hatch, who was eighty-nine years old. The bride, said the newspaper, was becomingly attired in a gown of white tulle, with white satin and lace trimmings. She carried a bouquet of roses and lilies of the valley. Under an arch of holly and Easter lilies the marriage was solemnized. Uncle Lisha and poor Uncle Ed were the ushers and Uncle Fred and a lady named Miss Warriner played the Lohengrin "Wedding March."

After a reception, the couple left for a week's honeymoon in New York and then went on to Baltimore, where Mama began a married life which turned out to be a little different from the kind most young ladies at that time undertook. For Father decided to become a mining engineer and soon after that Mama's education in packing and moving began.

There is no record of how many places they lived but my own first memory is of Colorado. Mama was wheeling me in one of those wicker baby carriages. I had on a lacy bonnet and fluffy frock (I hated to wear anything on my head even then). I was old enough to understand speech and I think able to walk on my own, but Mama had some distance to go and popped me in the carriage. A tall elegant lady stopped and bent over me and said to Mama, "Oh, what a beautiful child!"

She wore a lilac or lavender dress and a flowered hat. And the most delicious perfume drifted toward my eagerly sniffing nose. I suspect it may have been lavender for I have always loved it. The combination of the first words of praise I ever heard and the sweet delicate scent made an unforgettable experience.

My later memories of Colorado were also happy. Somehow Aunt Laura and her husband turned up along with their son, Edwin. Edwin Mather Duvall was my age and we played together in our yard all day long. This long-lasting love affair began quite naturally as we were very much alike. Perhaps that was why I never went through the traditional stage when girls hate boys and avoid any association with the strange opposite sex. Also it was the first time we had stayed in one place long enough for me to know any other child. Father was reasonably satisfied since he was teaching at the Colorado School of Mines and spent the summers prospecting. Edwin and I must have been six or seven.

One exciting day Edwin made a skeleton out of heavy paper and fixed it with strings so it jiggled and jumped up and down. A child psychologist might have predicted he would grow up to be a dedicated doctor but I only was awed at the production. He outlined bones in black crayon, and when he worked the strings it was certainly impressive enough to give me nightmares. I can still see it dancing in the bright Colorado sun.

I hated Father when he decided to move. But when we set up a tent in Tent City, California, my second love became the sea and I was happy. Father was an expert swimmer but Mama could not swim. Father took me into the ocean daily and I hung onto his shoulder as he plunged ahead. Then we walked on the beach while he told me about every seashell and how sand was made down through the ages and why the seaweed was there.

On the way back to the tent he usually bought a pailful of oranges and I ate oranges all day long. The rest of our diet was delicatessen food. I remember I found potato salad in a cardboard container delectable.

The next thing I knew we were in New Mexico, living in an adobe house which at least had walls and a real roof. The town was named Socorro and Father was at the School of Mines. We were there long enough for me to have a friend, a dark-eyed Mexican boy. I learned Mexican Spanish from him so we could chatter away, for he knew no English. We spent most of our time with my burro, Nellie. She would only go around and around the yard so that is where we rode. Once she livened things up by eating the entire washing off the line. Nellie was my first animal companion and to me she was beautiful.

Living was primitive in the tiny town but Father was

briefly happy. He had a black horse named Raylampego
(Lightning), and he rode to work wearing the garb of a
cowpuncher. One dusk he came riding back with two starving
baby lambs, one under each arm.

"I found them on the desert," he said. "They aren't
quite dead."

While Mama dug up a nursing bottle, Father carried
water from the well and heated it and gave them a bath.
They emerged soft and white as new snow.

We gave one to my Mexican friend and I kept the other
until it was nearly full grown. Then it disappeared mysteri-
ously one morning before I was awake. Father was gone, too,
and Mama would not tell me anything about it. When
Father came home that night, he said nothing about the
lamb, but I knew just the same, and I gave him a difficult
time. The expensive carom board he brought home did not
replace my lost pet.

During this period, Father was doing something I never
understood for the Paris Exhibition, and the house was piled
with scientific books and manuscripts belonging to the
French government. He often worked late at night and I
could see a glow from the oil lamp in the small front room.

One night I woke to see a blazing glow over everything
and to hear voices shouting outside, "Fire! Fire!" Mama
rushed in with her dark hair falling loose over her nightgown.
She swooped me up and ran to the door as Father unbolted
it. She thrust me into the arms of a Mexican woman in the
yard. I was carried to a two-room adobe house nearby and
tucked into a bunk in the main room. It was hot and smoky
there, and a bevy of Mexican children kept running up to
gabble about my blond hair. It was my first experience away
from home and from Mama, and I was in a frozen panic.

Strange men kept dashing through the room with buckets of water from the well out back. Some woman was in a corner crying.

I learned the rest of the story later and have told it often because the effect on our lives was lasting. The town was hot, dry and dusty, and our house burned down in about twenty minutes. Mama tried to save some clothes and Father attempted to save the French books and papers. The fire department had a hose wound around a homemade wheel and pulled by a couple of Mexican men but the hose could not reach as far as our well. At the last minute Father rushed back in and staggered out carrying a large square object in his blistered hands. He dropped it at Mama's feet and she stared in utter despair. It was the carom board.

When he saw it he was about to go in again and two of the men held him just as the roof fell. The carom board had stood against the wall under the portrait of Majel which was the same size and which he had had an artist neighbor paint sometime in the short six months of her life. It had a heavy gold frame with carving on it and whenever I looked at it I was filled with envy because I was not as beautiful as this rosy, blue-eyed, golden-haired baby. It was Father's most cherished possession.

Father burst into sobs and it took three men to keep him from going back into the wreckage. Dawn cast a pale light over the embers of the house and of the shed where Raylampego had died. He was always a fierce, high-spirited horse and none of the men had been able to get him out. All we had left was a few clothes Mama had saved and an elegant carom board.

"Rufus just lost his mind," Mama once told me.

At the moment, however, she had one more problem.

She did not have the faintest idea whom she had handed me over to. Nobody else seemed to know and Mama could not speak Spanish. Father spoke it fluently (much simpler than Greek and Latin, he said) but he could not be found. So Mama had to hunt for her missing daughter by going from house to house in the neighborhood. She found me at last, still wrapped in the blanket she had swept me up in, and being fed some tasty Mexican food which I had already developed a passion for.

The Bagg temperament has always been such that it has survived any disaster. It is not like the steady quiet strength of the Raybolds but is dramatically impressive. But Father gave up temporarily and Mama was terrified. He had lost the French government's priceless material; he had lost his beloved horse; he had lost Majel's portrait. Mama shed her tears in private over the loss of the wedding silver and all their furniture, clothing and bed linen. She tried to tell him all three of us were alive and safe and he did not even hear her words. He just wandered around in a daze.

He paid no attention to the minister. His faith in God was already shaky since Majel had gone, and this fire demolished it entirely, whereas Mama still took comfort in God.

In the end Mama held things together although now and then she had one of her sick headaches and went to bed with a damp cloth over her eyes. As for me, it was such a desolate period that I do not remember which of the few American families took us in. The New England relatives sent boxes of clothing and bedding. My favorite belongings were gone and somehow Nellie had vanished too. Mama had only her nightgown. Father had been fully dressed and his clothes were only singed here and there. Even his high-laced boots were all right and he must have grabbed his cartridge belt when the fire started so he still had his heavy revolver and hunting knife in its sheath.

One night after I was in bed Father came in and I heard him call for Mama. "We are going to leave," he said. "I have an offer to manage a silver mine. We can't stay here in this godforsaken place."

"Are we going back home?"

"No, we are going to Mexico," he said. Once more he sounded like himself. "It's in the Sierra Madre mountains."

On to Mexico

FATHER NEVER LOOKED HANDSOMER than when he took off for Mexico. His reddish curly hair was damp with sweat and no brushing flattened it. Under his wide brow his brilliant blue eyes shone with excitement. His typical Bagg skin, a clear delicate pink, was flushed. He had grown a mustache in order to look older and a neat half circle of reddish brush framed his eager sensitive mouth.

He wore his mining clothes and a new sombrero. His luggage consisted of a huge canvas bag with leather straps and a padlock. He also had an old square camera, with boxes of plates for it, and a tripod. His medicine case was black leather, opening out flat to reveal dozens of glass bottles filled with powders and pills. He felt he could cure himself and us of anything although he knew nothing about medicine.

When he boarded the creaky old train he drew a great deal of attention, especially from the few ladies already settled in. Mama and I watched the last trailing smoke, Mama pale and composed while I sobbed. We were to follow as soon as he found a place to live across the border.

We were parked in a dim boardinghouse in San Antonio. Mama had her money sewed into a linen pocket inside her corset. We stayed there about a month, instead of a week, and Mama spent most of her time hurrying to the telegraph office to see if a wire had come for her. The landlady decided Mama and I were abandoned and was ready to put us out the minute the money was gone. At night I could see Mama through the mosquito netting on my bed, just sitting at the window with her head in her hand and her lovely dark hair falling down over her nightgown.

At first Mama was too proud to wire Grandfather or Uncle Walter for help. When she had said the words "For better or worse," she believed in them. But finally the landlady gave notice that we were to leave at the end of the week. On Thursday night Mama put me to bed early. She was at last composing a wire to send back East. Suddenly the door banged open and Father exploded into the room and swept Mama into his arms while I tore at the mosquito netting, shouting with joy. Our hero had come back!

His face was coppery and tiny squinting wrinkles were around his eyes. His clothes were dusty but he wore a new sombrero with a real silver band. He had an armload of presents.

"Where have you been?" Mama wiped her eyes with her linen handkerchief.

"I had to stay at the mine," he explained. "It's ninety miles from the nearest village. I went by pack trail. I had lots of adventures. I'll tell you all about them. Now we better pack. We'll leave in the morning for Chihuahua. I found a place to live and it is fine. A Mexican family lives downstairs but we can use the patio."

His best adventure, it turned out, was spending a night at a mountain inn sitting up with his revolver ready while a couple of desperadoes fought in the next room. The landlord tried to persuade him to leave because he said gringos were not welcome in that area. Father said if they could draw any quicker than he could, he ought to be killed.

The house in Chihuahua was big and square and glaring white. There was a balcony and the rooms were much bigger than the adobe house. It was unfortunate that the Mexican family cleaned house just after we moved in and a phalanx of bedbugs came up to the balcony and invaded our quarters. In the morning I looked as if I had chicken pox. Father's confrontation with the Mexican family was held outside where Mama and I could not hear but he had no trouble communicating.

Mama went to bed with a sick headache, which was not eased by the cold wet cloth or the smelling salts. Father almost put us out of our misery permanently as he disinfected the place. It smelled for days. Then he found a downstairs flat and we moved out.

There we met an American woman named Mrs. Willis, who came over every day to see Mama and cry. Her husband was an engineer who was incommunicado in the jail for making some drawings that the police decided were the work of a spy.

Apparently our relations with the government of Mexico

were not very cozy at the time but the consul was doing his
best. Mrs. Willis, robed in black, spent her time calling on
the consul and coming to cry at our house. Mama was a
magnet for anyone in trouble and did what she could to encourage poor Mrs. Willis.

But when Mama came down with typhoid fever, the
visits stopped. (I never did learn whether Mr. Willis got out
of jail.) The one American doctor Father found explained
there were no hospital services available or any nurses. So
Father and I did our best, living mostly on bacon and eggs,
which he could cook. When Mama was delirious Father went
to pieces. Only Mama's determination not to leave us finally
triumphed. As soon as she began to recover Father was ready
to go back to the silver mine ninety miles away.

Most of the Americans were pulling out, for the talk of
revolution was growing and what government there was was
about to fall. A mine official brought a priest to our house
one day to talk to Father. It seemed Father had fired the
Mexican manager at the mine and the visitors wanted to
persuade him to leave the country before there was trouble.

That night a long brown arm pushed a black cloth
through the window bars. There was no question in Father's
mind about what it threatened. He put the lamp out without a sound. There was no sound outside either. After what
seemed an endless time, the cloth was slowly withdrawn. We
still sat trying not to breathe until Father spoke.

"They're gone."

"Rufus, let's go home," whispered Mama.

"Nobody is going to drive me out," said Father.

He cleaned and loaded his revolver and from that time
on, he kept it with him. Whenever he went out we expected
never to see him again. Fortunately the mine closed down

soon after that so Father could leave with dignity and leave alive.

"We'll come back as soon as this mess is over," he said. "Those mountains are loaded with silver."

Mama was packing boxes. She straightened up and faced him.

"Rufus Mather Bagg," she said, "if you don't stop this wandering around I am going back to Massachusetts and make a home for our child."

For once in his life Father was unable to speak.

It was Mama's one rebellion, on behalf of their only remaining offspring. Nobody can ever know whether she would actually have left him and gone back to Massachusetts. I myself doubt that she would have. However, her ultimatum meant that I grew up with two parents instead of one and I am grateful, for my love for Father was passionate and my love for Mama was as basic as the marrow in my bones.

Occasionally I have told some of these happenings and written about them, but it was not until years later that I began to think about that period. My thoughts are confused as I wonder about Father and Mama and their marriage. Did Mama ever regret not marrying gentle Uncle Ed and spending her life safely by the placid Connecticut River? Would Majel and Walter have lived and, instead of being raised as an only child, would I have had a sister and a brother? Would I have been less lonely?

I always come back to a firm realization that my parents loved each other with a kind of until-death-do-us-part intensity that is no longer common. I think about them often in these days of quick divorces and when I listen to women's lib members. If I try to imagine what either of them would say about these things, I am helpless. I do not think Father ever bothered about belonging to the superior sex, for he assumed it. And in her quiet way, Mama would have simply remarked, "A woman's place is with her husband." Today Father might be ready to move to Alaska to study glaciers. Or to plunge through rain forests looking for lost tribes, for he loved anthropology. Or to go on a real safari in Africa. He lived completely from day to day. And Mama, I think, would have lived each day with him no matter where.

In any case, we went back to Illinois, where Father accepted a position as an instructor of geologoy at the University. We lived in a real house on a shady, quiet street and I went to school. What I remember best is sitting under a giant mock orange bush in the backyard trying to write poetry, a kind of solace, for I was lonely.

I was an alien. I had to learn about life in an American town. I had to forget the Mexican Spanish I spoke more easily than my own language. And I had to realize that I knew a good many things the rest of the children in my class did not, but I knew nothing about so many things they had learned coming up the normal way in grade school. I was terrified when I had to speak in class.

I also knew if I received less than A plus—or I think they called it 98—I would have a fearsome session with my father when I brought my report home.

Fortunately in summer Father went off locating artesian wells and doing geological surveys and Mama and I went back to Grandfather's in Massachusetts. There were countless cousins and the farm itself was full of delights. I had my second friend, my cousin Christine, and about the only thing we did separately was brush our teeth.

Life at Grandfather's house was easy. Grandma spent most of her time playing the Steinway grand piano in the drawing room. Bridget cooked and served meals that were

epic. Breakfast was bacon and eggs, pancakes with homemade maple syrup, fried sugar-cured ham, hot biscuits, usually
topped off with apple pie. I gained weight, which at that
time was a fine idea for I was so thin Father called me the
starving Belgian.

Christine and I walked freely anywhere on the land. In
the tall rows of sweet-scented corn we ran up and down
hunting for Indian arrowheads. We went swimming in the
Connecticut River at the edge of Uncle Ed's land. We
sneaked into the icehouse, which was strictly forbidden. On
a hot summer day we buried our toes in the damp, cool saw-
dust and broke off slivers of ice to suck. We were only caught
once and were punished by being sent to our rooms for half
a day.

We also slipped into the medicine closet off the dining
room at Grandfather's. It was a narrow, long room with green
and gold stained-glass windows. The ranks of patent medicines rose to the ceiling. We never touched the bottles but
loved to read the labels. They cured everything from female
complaints to inflammation of the bowels. Doctors were only
called if some child fell out of an apple tree and broke a
bone.

In a household in which spirits were never allowed, the
alcoholic content of many of the medicines ran as high as
18 percent and certainly eased some ailments. Every family
in that area also made herb infusions which worked remark-
ably well on a number of complaints. Either because of or in
spite of that mysterious room's array of bottles, the Bagg
family was incredibly healthy.

Everyone was musical. In the evening the drawing room
was filled with children and adults all either singing or playing some instrument. It was my introduction to a passion
that has never left me. Even Father sang in his cheerful

moments when he was there to take us back to the Midwest. His clear, powerful tenor soared above everything and his three brothers and four sisters added depth and extra beauty as Grandma rippled away on the grand piano. Between songs, they argued passionately as to what to sing next and what key to sing it in.

Most of them played several instruments. Mostly they sang opera. Father had put away his violin when Majel died but Uncle Lisha filled in.

Sometime during that period Aunt Ida married a wealthy man. The wedding was spectacular. The bride wore white satin, draped in folds and gathered at the waist. There was crepe de chine somehow mixed with it, but I cannot imagine how! She had a long court train and the veil reached to the bottom of the train. The waist was ornamented with beads. She carried a bouquet of roses and sweet peas tied with maline. Aunt Minnie, the newspaper reported, was "matron of honor." She wore yellow crepe de chine and carried pink Killarney roses. (There must be an error in the faded news clipping since Aunt Minnie never married. She had a single romance in her youth and remained faithful to the memory ever after.)

The wedding supper was served for two hundred guests afterward. The newspaper reported, "The couple received a number of attractive and useful gifts." The bridegroom gave Aunt Ida a diamond pendant set in platinum and she gave him a diamond stickpin and two Liberty bonds. The wedding party received pins set with diamonds and pearls or pearl and sapphire pins.

Grandfather must have been happy to provide a wedding for a daughter who married properly and did not elope!

But my favorite description of this event comes from my cousin Rob, who was then five or six. He insists he was nothing but a flower girl. He wore what he says is a kind of white frock and carried a basket of roses to strew ahead of the bride. He still reddens like a boiled lobster when he recalls his misery.

I am also impressed with Aunt Ida giving her bridegroom two Liberty bonds. I doubt whether this could happen today, especially if the groom was more than affluent. It shows, I think, that she inherited Grandfather's sense of money.

The summer visits to Grandfather's went on for several years, and I was a happy child, being part of a big family and having the free run of a farm. Years later these memories were chiefly responsible for my acquiring thirty-one acres (more or less as the deed said) of New England farmland with a 1690 farmhouse set in the midst of it.

I must, before closing this period, speak of Grandfather. He was the typical Bagg, short, stocky, incredibly powerful. He did not look like a farmer but rather a banker. His exuberant curly hair was white as new snow, as was his flowing beard. He had the brilliant blue eyes set under a wide forehead; the firm, straight nose of the Mather heritage; and, from what you could see of it, a sensitive mouth. For years I accepted him as the image of God and even now I wonder if God does not look exactly like Grandfather!

He ran his world like a kingdom, stern but just. When he sat at the head of the huge dining table, he viewed his eight offspring with a searching look and woe to anyone who failed in manners. There was no giggling at that table or any misbehavior. He carved the rich, juicy roast beef expertly. His hands were square but with long fingers, the middle one being especially long. His wrists were flexible so that the hands moved with grace.

Grandmother was a guest at the table. She also had curly hair, pinned up on top of her head, and sea-blue eyes. But she had a smiling mouth and crinkles of laughter around the eyes. I never saw her troubled or upset. She seemed to wear life lightly. She was always dressed in a soft gown with full sleeves and lace around the throat. This was pinned with an elegant brooch.

We were all in awe of Grandfather but Grandmother had a lap meant for sitting on. She was the one to run to if we stepped on a rusty nail or had upset the bees in one of the beehives by poking a stick in to try to get honey.

The custom of the times is reflected in a faded photograph of the two of them. Grandfather sits in a high-backed carved chair with a look of quiet majesty. Grandmother stands a little behind him with her arms folded behind her back and a gentle smile on her rosy face. On the back of the photograph, in what must be his definite, forceful handwriting, the caption reads, "Rufus Mather Bagg." Below this it says simply, "Wife."

It seemed natural to all of us to have the whole establishment focus around Grandfather. When he went to New York to sit on the Stock Exchange, the house fell into confusion, rudderless. Grandmother was not born to be an executive. Bridget ran the establishment while Grandmother played the piano and often sang in a sweet soprano voice. Sometimes I had the feeling she was not really noticing anything but was just waiting for Grandfather to come back and pick up the reins again.

Even after he had an automobile, he preferred to come from the station in the buggy drawn by his favorite white horses. He strode into the house, walking rapidly but with dignity. He greeted his wife with a formal embrace but I do not remember him ever kissing the children. We greeted him with proper respect and then rushed out of doors to act like wild Indians, as Grandmother said.

The only summer during those years that was not a golden haze of days was the summer we visited Uncle Walter in Pittsfield.

I came down with scarlet fever almost at once. For six weeks Mama and I lived in an upstairs bedroom with a sheet soaked daily in carbolic acid tacked over the door. Food was brought upstairs on trays which were left by the door. Mama waited until the sound of footsteps diminished down the long curving staircase and then crept out far enough to bring the trays in. The doctor came in now and then and he smelled heavily of disinfectant. Since I am very sensitive to odors, I still remember the strong smell of the carbolic acid and of the disinfectant.

During this time my second favorite cousin in Riverdale died of scarlet fever and I heard the announcement from someone poking a nose around the sheet at the door. I had nightmares after that.

When she wasn't waiting on me, Mama sat at the window overlooking the canopy of green leaves outside, as she wrote to Father. In those days you lived or died without help from antibiotics. When my fever was high, she sponged me with cold water, and when the sheets were soaked with sweat, she rolled me from one side to the other in bed while she changed them and then worked me into a clean nightgown. The sheets were boiled the next day. Everyone agreed that scarlet fever was highly contagious and that was all they knew.

When I was well enough to sit up in bed, Uncle Walter brought me a jigsaw puzzle of a big ship, which I loved. I had some books to read but the puzzle was my treasure.

When the day finally came that I was out of danger to myself and my poor mother, we were packed up and sent back to the Midwest as fast as possible. Everything in the room except the furniture was burned. I begged and wept about the ship puzzle. I kept saying, "It has a separate piece for a porthole!" But my puzzle went into the fire along with the bedding, the books and everything movable. We had the clothes we wore and a suitcase of underwear which was brand new.

There was no real farewell. The family waved at us through the parlor windows as we rode off in a buggy to the station. I know Aunt Grace was relieved to see us go and probably expressed herself to Uncle Walter about his relatives ever coming again to visit, and I know we never did!

When we got home, Father was back from some expedition and angry about the whole thing. I was so thin and pale. Mama looked as if she had been put through a wringer. He had to blame someone and he decided my poor cousin had given me the disease and we should not have been in New England anyway.

Then he explained to Mama he had been offered a position as head of the geology department at Lawrence College in Appleton, Wisconsin. He was tired of working under someone. It was too hot in Illinois and he suffered from the heat. We were to pack up and go. He already had a house rented in Appleton. It was all going to be wonderful and also he had in his contract that he could go off on geological projects when he wanted to. He already had one lined up— finding enough artesian water for some paper company.

So Mama packed again.

The House
by the River

FATHER BUILT A HOUSE on top of a steep bank overlooking the Fox River. Then we had a permanent address: 16 Brokaw Place. Father himself was the architect. He also helped the builder so much that Mama was privately asked if she could keep him away more of the time.

It was a big square stucco house and way ahead of its time, as most of Father's projects were. The spacious living room had picture windows overlooking the river and a glassed-in sunporch extended beyond it. There was a large dining room and a kitchen with built-in cabinets, a breakfast nook and a gas stove with the oven perched on top near the ceil-

ing. A bathroom and Father's study opened into the front
hall where the huge staircase wound to the upstairs.

The piano was at one end of the living room. Most of
the walls had built-in bookcases with cabinets at the bottom
for books which would not fit in the shelves. The fireplace
was tawny brick and had the family coat of arms embedded
in it over the hearth. Three rampant lions, or griffins, guarded
the shield and its message, "*Virtus vera nobilitas est.*" Father
firmly believed that virtue is the true nobility.

Upstairs were two big bedrooms, and a bath the size of
my current kitchen. A smaller bedroom with the elegance of
a toilet bowl and hot and cold running water was intended
for Grandma Raybold when she came to live with us, which
she never did. Mama turned it into a sewing room eventually.
Over the sunporch there was a sleeping porch that opened
from the master bedroom. Father was a fresh-air addict and
many a night when it was twenty below poor Mama left the
warm, coal-heated interior of the house to crawl in shivering
beside her husband on that sleeping porch. She wrapped
herself in sweaters and Father wore his long underwear under his nightshirt.

Often I woke up to hear her pedaling away at the sewing machine in the warm room always called "Grandma
Raybold's." Father slept heavily but if he did wake up and
find her gone, he let his unhappiness be known.

A room of my own, a room with my very own furniture
and a view of the river, added up to a piece of heaven. I could
turn on a lamp and write what I assumed was poetry while
a silver moon walked the sky over the river.

What impressed visitors, actually, was the cellar, which
was built as solid as an Egyptian pyramid, with cement but-
tresses, double thick walls, a seven-inch or more cement floor

and a separate root cellar. The coal bin was adequate for a hotel.

Mama's domain was the kitchen, of course. Mr. Lutz, the iceman, brought huge cakes of ice through the back door and gentled them into the icebox. As soon as electric refrigerators came in, Father got one. Then I missed watching Mr. Lutz drive up in the ice wagon drawn by two white horses. I could always go out on an August day and scoop up a handful of ice slivers. Mama also had one of the first fireless cookers, which consisted of a square, tall, insulated metal box into which you put soapstone units that had been heated on the gas range. Baked beans, left in overnight, were the best in the world.

The overall impression was one of luxury. Father made friends with the Oriental rug dealer and we walked on Orientals. There were drapes on the downstairs windows and deep-pile carpeting on the stairs.

Outside in the driveway stood the automobile, which was a Keeton, supposed to be a French car. It was the only one in town with wire spokes on the wheels and a sloping hood. It was ahead of its time, just as Father was. It was an open touring car but had side curtains with isinglass panels in case of rain. By the time they had been buttoned in, Father was soaked, and if you were inside you looked through those panels at a wavy, murky world for they were not like the clear plastic we see nowadays.

About this time, incidentally, Uncle Lisha tried to start an automobile factory and produced a car he designed himself. It was too advanced in construction so he went bankrupt and his partner vanished with what assets they had.

Also at this time our friend and family physician, Dr. Ritchie, hung up the old harness, bridle and blanket and drove a Cartercar in the barn after making house calls all over the countryside. He always said his horse was more reliable, for his car had a habit of stalling on bitter winter nights.

Our best friends, the Russells, had a big sedan which was a Cadillac, I believe. It was famous for having thirty flat tires when we made a one-day round trip in both cars to The Dells, a beautiful unspoiled river gorge. Also the radiator kept boiling over so we stopped at almost every farmhouse and lugged water from the well. When a tire went flat, the men jacked the wheel up, put on a patch, and then pumped the tire up with a hand pump while the families stood around sweating in heavy dusters. We wore thick goggles and scarves over our heads but the unpaved dirt roads laid a coating of dust over us anyway.

In winter we carried tire chains since nobody had heard of snow tires. However, there were advantages for drivers in those days. Parking was no problem at all. Roads were never crowded and gas flowed freely. When we went camping, which we did often, we never looked for a state camping area. We pulled off the road anywhere by a lake or trout stream. I am still in awe of the state parks with hookups for electricity and running water and with restrooms as well as picnic tables. We took jugs of water with us and all our supplies, including lanterns. The tent was tied on top of the Keeton and the folding cots rode in the backseat. Father built two heavy black wooden boxes for the running boards, which gave us the appearance of carrying two coffins. They held groceries and extra clothing, an ax, hammers, saws, shovel and extra boots.

Mama and I took a dim view of these trips since they were so much work and so uncomfortable. We did not care

for nights in a damp tent with mosquito netting swathed
around us and strange noises from wildlife snuffling around
looking for handouts. It usually rained the entire time, but
even if it didn't, the tent never seemed to dry out. We were
scared of snakes while Father enjoyed proving his marksman-
ship by shooting their heads off.

If we were by a clear, sparkling lake we could go swimming but otherwise we bathed in a washbasin. Mama heated
water on a camp stove and washed out our clothes.

The house on Brokaw Place always looked like a castle
to us when we got home. Mama cooked up a storm in her
kitchen and we had hot baths and slept in big, comfortable
beds not draped with mosquito netting. Both of us prayed
that Father would be content to stay put, as Mama said, and
if he took off the black boxes from the running boards we
were happy. Mama found extra chores for him to do, hoping
he would not be restless for a while.

Fortunately much of the summer he could still do artesian well work, make geological surveys and so on, although
he had no silver mine to run. He was seldom away for more
than a few days at a time, and since we now had a home of
our own, Mama and I stayed right there. I missed the visits
to Grandfather's, though, and Mama allowed me to write
Uncle Ed and ask for a permanent loan of Christine. He
had six children and was always in financial difficulties since
he lacked Grandfather's genius for farming as well as his
shrewd business sense.

I wrote a number of sad, lonely letters but Uncle Ed
would not send Christine out. Father did his best and
promised Uncle Ed he would see Christine through college,
but nothing worked.

Meanwhile I worked daily on Father to get me an Irish

setter. Aside from Nellie and the lamb, I never had a pet except, very briefly, an American water spaniel. I dreamed of an Irish, although I had never seen one except in a picture somewhere. I suspect Father got tired of my bringing home paper bags filled with newborn kittens that had been tossed into an alley which was a shortcut from school. They all died and he grew tired of my "carrying on."

One birthday he was planning to buy me a diamond ring. It must have been my first year in high school when I had managed to get a decent grade in mathematics for the first time. Father said we did not want a large, unsanitary dog running around the house. Our confrontation, as people now call it, went on for some time. I said I did not want any old diamond ring; I wanted an Irish setter. We were enough alike so that Mama had a hard time. It was Greek meeting Greek—in spades.

His name was Timothy Pepper and he came from Minnesota from a Mr. Pepper's kennel. In those days, pedigreed dogs were not common, and in our town I doubt whether anyone had ever seen an Irish.

Timmie came by train in a big wooden crate with air holes punched in it. You could smell the crate all over the station as the man unloaded him from the baggage car. He was half starved, his deep mahogany coat clotted with filth. At six weeks he was mostly paws and tail (which was only a ratlike appendage then). He flung himself in my arms as soon as the crate was pried open and I cried while he slobbered with joy.

He was registered as Timothy Mather Pepper, and after Mama scrubbed him and me both, he began fourteen years of managing the household. Father had a typewritten sheet of paper with rules for his behavior. But Timmie made his own. Father built a house for him big enough to accommodate a giraffe so he could sleep outside the house. Timmie preferred sleeping with his head on my pillow. Timmie spent part of one night in his house and that was all. He kept the neighbors awake until even Father was aroused.

The first few nights he slept on a very fine bed in the kitchen. I got up after Father was snoring away on the sunporch and Timmie and I snugged down in my bed. By the time Father found out, Mama intervened in her quiet way and the doghouse made pretty good fireplace wood.

Timmie had no problems with Mama. If he wanted to go out, he began playing with his ball until he rolled it under the big radiator in the living room. Then Mama had to drop whatever she was working at and fish out his ball, at which point he rushed to the front door.

As long as you are up anyway, he said plainly. It never failed.

When he wanted to come back in, he stood on tiptoes and began clawing at the back door, barking loud enough to wake an Egyptian mummy.

He became a town character, known everywhere as Dr. Bagg's dog. He had a regular route for visiting friends, always turning up at Connie Johnson's the morning she made fresh doughnuts, which he loved. He dropped in at the Ritchies daily and once dug under the barn after a rat and got stuck. It took Dr. Ritchie and Father quite a time to shovel him out. The following day he came home with a toy telephone tied around his neck. "So he can call up when he needs you," said the doctor.

Of course he met a skunk and even scrubbing in the laundry tub in the cellar did not do much good. A week later all of us still had an unmistakable odor. When he got involved with a porcupine, the doctor got the quills out.

"That will teach you," said Father.

One summer he developed a skin eczema. The local veterinarian—called the Cow Doctor—had no success with the usual salves and ointments so at last he tried changing Timmie's diet. Among other things, he prescribed oatmeal. Mama cooked it overnight in the fireless cooker, and since there was a lot of it, we all ate it for breakfast, although neither Timmie nor I liked oatmeal. Father ate it happily as long as he also had bacon and eggs or pancakes and maple syrup, plus a wedge of apple pie. I don't think the oatmeal could have helped Timmie but the eczema cleared up anyway.

Timmie liked to help out the family by bringing home roast beef or pork from neighbors' back porches. In those days butchers delivered orders and if the lady of the house was away left them at the kitchen door. There were no names on the packages, for the butcher knew very well who had ordered what. Timmie would bring them home without a damp spot on them and lay them at Mama's feet. Mama spent a good deal of time phoning around to find out who was missing the meat for supper (it was only "dinner" on Sunday or when one entertained).

It is a tribute to Timmie that when she timidly explained that we had a leg of lamb, which Timmie delivered, the answer was always the same. "Oh, good. I thought it might have been stolen. Can you send Gladys over with it?"

Naturally, if Timmie took it, it was not really stealing!

Father could never admit how much he loved this Irish. But Timmie took to following him to the campus and seeing him safely inside of Science Hall. Often he met him when classes were over and escorted him home. Then came the day Father had to lead chapel, despite his valiant efforts to escape it. He appeared in his academic robes with the beau-

tiful blue velvet hood, and when he was thus attired he was
no longer my father but an imposing figure. In the middle
of the first prayer, one creature who was not awed came
trotting down the aisle and leaped to the pulpit and sat
down by Father, wagging ecstatically. That was a chapel
service nobody ever forgot! After the benediction, the president rose and addressed the students.

"If all of you would behave as well as Dr. Bagg's dog,"
he said in resonant tones, "I think the college would be better off!"

Timmie's fame was nearly his undoing because he loved
riding in a car. One day someone picked him up and went
off with him. I have related this episode often, and the suffering of those next four days is still fresh in my mind. The
whole town turned out to hunt and we kept at it night and
day. The *Post Crescent* made appeals. The fourth day a
farmer who lived forty miles out in the country called up to
say he had an Irish setter with a chewed rope around his
neck, and could it be Dr. Bagg's!

One Small Town

Now THAT THE SMALL TOWN is vanishing a good many authors have written about it, as well as about the joys of country living. Many also write about life in the wilderness where man can really get back to nature, untamed and unspoiled.

So I, too, think about my own small town of Appleton before it became a city. What was then Lawrence College is now the University with all the extra advantages but without the small tree-shaded campus and old, ivy-covered grey stone buildings. In spring, the light was green from new leaves making a canopy over the walks. In autumn, the lawns lay deep in russet and gold leaves.

The college campus fronted on Main Street and was the central point of the town. The chapel was across the street, and very beautiful it seemed to us. The president's house was at one side of the main campus, solid and gracious. Main Hall was in the center, Science Hall behind it.

Since students either walked or rode bicycles, there were no drab expanses for parking automobiles. There were just enough driveways by the buildings to provide parking for the professors who owned cars.

The business section stretched along Main Street with the grocer's, butcher shop, Pettibone's department store, a shoe cobbler, a small movie house and a beauty shop where one could get permanent waves. The dentist and the drugstore were there as well as Conkey's Book and Stationery store. Mr. Conkey carried a few books but refused to stock any of Edna Ferber's. She came from Appleton and he had never liked her. To get a Ferber book, you had to order from Milwaukee or Chicago. I could never reach Mr. Conkey myself but someone told me he disliked the whole Ferber family. Perhaps he had bought something from Mr. Ferber's clothing store and did not like it!

The only hospital was St. Mary's at the edge of town. The railroad station was across town at the opposite edge. The high school was set beyond the residential district, possibly three miles from Brokaw Place. There were no buses. We walked to school and back.

The residential area was green with shade in summer, deep with snow in winter. The houses belonged to the Victorian era, with comfortable front porches and bright gardens. Behind most were barns left over from the horse and buggy days, with vegetable patches flourishing in front of them.

The Fox River was wide and sweet as it flowed around

the town. Winding paths led to it here and there and one enterprising man had a kind of shack on the bank where he rented out canoes and rowboats. This was simply called "downriver."

In the distance the first sign of progress was visible, the Kimberly Clark paper mill. Its only offense was to fill the air with the pungent smell of sulfur, much like hard-boiled eggs which have stood around too long. The water tasted of the sulfur, too. It was a cause of complaint year in and year out, but I loved it. Some people bought bottled water but we never did.

The telephone service was typical of a nonmechanized age. The phones hung on the wall and you wound up a crank to get the operator. Then, after a short visit with her, you gave your number.

"Oh, she's gone to a church meeting," you might hear. "She will be back around five."

Or, "Poor Mr. Gregory was taken to the hospital this morning with a pain in his chest."

The operators were persons and friends. They were a kind of answering service, infinitely better than the recorded messages one gets these days. And nobody ever said that you had the wrong number. They got you the correct one and then hooked you up.

Heating problems were solved simply. Woodburning stoves had gone out, except in some kitchens, and furnaces kept houses warm even at thirty below zero. They burned coal and the man of the house shoveled it in regularly. Hot-water radiators were good for drying damp mittens and boots. Sometimes Father "bled" ours by taking off the metal gadget at one end and letting some water run into an empty coffee can.

One time he nearly burned the house down by trying to start the furnace with a swig of kerosene which turned out to be gasoline. Furnaces were slow to start in the fall but their mechanism was so simple they almost never went out.

Almost everything was delivered, not only the meat but fresh, rich milk, big country brown eggs, butter and cottage cheese. The mailman blew his horn or whistle at the gate or carried packages to the front door. The paper boys rode bicycles and came along after school.

There were no Laundromats but most women had washing machines with hand wringers attached, and clothes blew on clotheslines to dry.

There was a period when escape from small towns was a popular subject among writers and the object of many people's struggle. The free horizons beckoned, promising a life less restricted than in the hometown. I notice that nostalgia now blooms like daffodils in spring for those same small towns. For a good many people, the congested, air-polluted, noisy metropolis, the cramped apartment existence and the jammed subways and scarce taxis have all brought on a kind of fatigue.

Life patterns in a small town were regimented. You went to church. You belonged to clubs. Mama's club was the Clio Club, meeting for tea and watercress sandwiches or cakes and reading Dickens aloud. Men had fraternal organizations. The ladies never intruded on the gentlemen's clubs.

There was none of what could be called nightlife. At night, people usually went to bed early. Occasionally in our college town there were concerts or lectures from various experts who were sent from a lecture bureau. There were church suppers; there were strawberry festivals and skating parties. The college senior prom and the high school class dances were special occasions. College and high school football games were memorable events, too. A few men played chess and there were some couples who gathered for bridge games.

Most yards had croquet sets. After a fried chicken and homemade ice cream dinner, young and old played croquet. There were no cocktail parties but plenty of luncheons and teas and picnics.

What made the small town different went deeper than the mechanics of living. It was a sense of community. There was something organic about it, I think, perhaps the last heritage from the tribe or clan. It was highly personal and this sometimes was a disadvantage, for gossip flourished and feuds could be bitter.

Years later when I had to live in New York City, I was amazed that in a big apartment building one could live indefinitely without knowing the names of the other residents. Now I see, in the apartment-house associations which have sprung up, an attempt to recapture some of that communal sense.

It is interesting that small-town life provided much less privacy in the midst of far more space. Wide green lawns, garden plots, overarching trees gave a sense of freedom. Even across the railroad tracks in the poorer section, houses were set apart sufficiently so nobody looked into the next-door kitchen or heard the phonograph playing, "I Want a Girl Just Like the Girl Who Married Dear Old Dad." (Freud was not yet in vogue.) Yet there was no chance of leading a secret life, for there were no secrets. Everybody knew everybody, what they were doing and where they went.

In our small midwestern town the bitter black and white racial conflict had not arisen, merely because of the location.

An occasional black family might turn up, although I do
not remember any. This rich farming country was settled in
early times by pioneers pushing west as they wished. The
slave society of the South was so far away, few were even
conscious of it. Germans, Swedes, Norwegians, a few Polish,
a few Irish and later a small Jewish contingent made up the
ethnic groups, along with New England Yankees.

Mama's dearest friend was Mrs. Novak, who was a cleaning woman. When she came skipping up the walk we were
all happy. She was slight and dark-haired and her eyes shone
like polished jet. She was starched to the last apron string.
I knew vaguely that she had family troubles, which she shared
with Mama over a cup of tea, but I was never allowed to
listen.

Then there was Alma Albrecht. She was typically German with fair skin and wide blue eyes and a generous mouth.
She was the sewing lady and lived in a pleasant house across
town. Her sister, Irene, taught music. Her younger brother,
Carl, was in high school with me and had a hard time fend-
ing off the girls, including me.

The sewing lady was an institution at that time. Ready-
made clothes from Pettibone Peabody were available but a
large portion of ladies' and children's clothes were made at
home. Mama herself was an expert seamstress, even to the
point of making herself a brown tailored suit, but Alma always turned up to help fit, to turn up hems and eventually to
make my wedding dress and veil.

Alma usually brought us homemade noodles when she
came, rich, pale golden, and I fell on them like a hungry
wolf. She also made stollen and sauerkraut and Christmas
cookies.

A few of the wealthy folk occasionally went to Milwaukee or even Chicago to shop for clothes although it was a long, tiresome trip on the sooty train.

The men usually bought their clothes at the small men's clothing store or had them made by the local tailor. They wore sober suits and white shirts with starched collars. Father was a shade radical when he got a winter overcoat with a fur collar. Shoes were just shoes. They were polished black or brown, usually laced.

Jewelry was reserved for the ladies, but men were permitted elegant cufflinks and gold watches with gold chains. A few men did wear wedding bands. Tie pins could be indulged in.

Ladies wore earrings in their pierced ears. Pearls were popular, as were diamond rings, amber beads, gold chains with cameos attached, watches with jewels in the clips that fastened above gentle bosoms. Gold or silver bracelets set with jewels were for parties.

I think there is one thing in today's world Father would have approved of—male fashions. He would have loved bright-colored trousers, checked shirts open at the neck, full flaring ties and a little finger ring, set with one of his precious stones. The soft, flexible, moccasin type of footwear would have made his sensitive feet comfortable but he would not have gone as far as sandals!

In the deep Wisconsin winters both sexes wore heavy galoshes or fur-lined boots. They were usually buckled neatly, although I always flapped around with mine unbuckled.

Winter clothing for men, women and children was old-fashioned woolen. Synthetics had not yet appeared on the horizon. Wool was soft and warm but could not be tossed into the washing machine and run through the hand wringer.

Mackinaws were a staple, most of them with heavy hoods

attached. Gloves were leather, fur-lined at times, or thick
wool. Then there were the mufflers, also for men and women,
and how I hated to wear a muffler! Ear muffs were fur or
wool.

Even in January no ladies wore warm slacks. For skating
they had long, full woolen skirts with warm blouses under
their solid jackets. Sometimes they carried muffs.

This was far enough back in time so that wearing fur
was ethical. Nobody gave a thought to wildlife. Mama had
a mink muff and a seal coat, and the thought of it horrifies
me now. Father gave me an Alaskan seal coat to take to college, which he bought from the furrier in Berlin, and which
I am sad to say I never thought of as meaning the death of
baby seals.

Then there were fur lap robes. Our doctor had one for
those long rides at night to outlying farms. So even Dr.
Ritchie contributed to the diminution of our precious wildlife!

Most of the men in our town were not the kind to make
a game of killing, like British fox hunters or American hunters
who kill for sport. But many of them hunted at times, bringing home just one deer for venison, and most of them went
fishing in the nearby rivers and lakes.

So life went on in the town along the river. There were
tragedies but they did not make headlines in the *Post Crescent*. There were a few suicides ("She had not been feeling
well") and some miserable marriages ("Poor Mrs. Carter,
she has a hard time") and some scandals ("He was seen with
that woman at ten o'clock at night"). But it was a time when
nobody worried about finding himself or herself. People were
too busy living.

I know small towns are doomed, not only from my own

experience with three of them but also from reading so much on the subject. The personal aspect is more moving than the statistics, as I discovered recently when a dear friend from Virginia wrote that her family's gracious old mansion had been razed to provide a parking lot. I used to visit there and I remember it well, with its green lawns and flower-filled garden. I felt the reassurance of the past in those big high-ceilinged rooms, with the curving staircase, the flowers filling the air with sweetness. Now where the roses grew, asphalt marks their grave. Magnolias and lilacs are gone. The house itself was chopped away, although perhaps someone saved some of the paneling. The parking lot accommodates about eighty cars; the tentacles of today reach out like an octopus to swallow yesterday.

Someday Father's house, with its bastions of cement underneath and its massive walls, will be flattened. I hope no kind friend will write and tell me. In my memory it is there and I do not think anything is lost as long as it lives in memory.

Also I do not believe in despair. Some communities still try to preserve their identity and I think this struggle increases. In Appleton we had a small sect of Millerites, who knew Judgment Day was coming soon and even which day it was. One night they dressed in white robes like nightgowns and spent all night on the roof of a house not far from ours, waiting for the world to be destroyed and they themselves to be swept up to heaven.

We used to walk by that house and wonder how they felt when the next day the milkman came along as usual! When I remember them, I decide not to anticipate, but, like Father, to live day by day.

And So Live Ever

MY PERSONAL LIFE began in the house by the river. Today's teenagers have horizons we never dreamed of. Drama groups go to England and youth choirs and orchestras tour Romania. Other students go to Greece or Italy or Switzerland. One exchange student in my family went to India and lived with an Indian family even before she went to college.

Many go to Washington, often on marches for various causes. They seem to spend almost as much time in the air as on the ground. And they know more about politics and the world situation than most government leaders.

All that I and my friends knew was that there were two

parties in the United States but the Republican party was
the one to vote for. Local politics had no meaning. I never
knew how my town was run. There must have been the usual
Town Fathers, there was a police department which did not
have much to do, and there was a school board to make
rules for the grade school and high school.

The high school was one of the best. It was a big, ugly
building set at the edge of town. It had no swimming pool,
no tennis courts. The gymnasium was small and simple.
Classrooms were plain square or rectangular rooms. The auditorium was large enough for all public activities, including
the senior play and graduation. There were no physics labora-
tories and no lounging rooms. The football field was simply a
vacant plot of land nearby, usually knee-deep in mud or thick
with dust. A stand of plain, open bleachers was on one side.
When it rained or snowed the audience put on rain hats and
rubber raincoats. We either walked to school or rode bicycles. We walked to the football field. Any modern teen-
ager would be horrified at the whole setup of the school.
There was not even a cafeteria serving hot lunches.

But we had the one thing that makes education exciting.
We had a group of the most gifted teachers I have ever
known. We also had an academic curriculum with no frills.
We had a student body with a single purpose, to learn all
they could and to get good grades.

This may have been due to the fact that some parents and
most grandparents who settled in this town had never had
enough education and revered it beyond measure. Or possibly the fact that it was the home of an excellent small midwestern college made a difference. I do not know. In any
case, dropouts occurred only when some boy had to stay
home to help on the farm because of an emergency. Those

we now call underachievers did the best they could to graduate even with C minus, and the teachers were never too busy to give extra tutoring. There were no drug problems then, no vandalism that I can remember, no student protests. We belonged to an age of acceptance.

We learned out of books and from the teachers, without benefit of the many modern visual aids. We took our report cards home proudly or with cold chills. In occasional sessions in the auditorium, the sturdy, square-set principal tried to inspire us to further efforts to learn.

We took the courses we were supposed to, whether we liked the subject or not. Therefore we had no real independence. But we had Calla Guyles in Latin and Lucrezia Van Zandt in algebra and a German teacher who made that language as rich as a ripened peach.

Physical education was an afterthought. The girls' basketball team wore serge bloomers and white middies. We had relay races in the football field and invariably I came in last. The boys had football and basketball and racing. Most of our sports we taught ourselves—skating, iceboating, swimming, tennis (we used the college courts for this). There was an old building in town where roller skating was brought in, and in winter we went roller skating.

The high school dances were held in the gymnasium. Sweet fruit punch with strawberries floating in the bowl was served, along with cookies or tea cakes. Students wore their Sunday clothes and were polite to the chaperones. Waltzes and fox-trots were popular but there was one very gay dance in which the partner swung you around in the air and that was my favorite.

The music the school band or orchestra provided was not ear-splitting. It was possible to talk to one's partner or hum the numbers. I cannot keep in tune but I loved to sing "Moonlight Bay" or "Sweetheart of Sigma Chi" or "You Can't Stop Me from Lovin' You."

After the dance couples walked home in the moonlight and said good night with a brief kiss and a hug. It was not a real embrace as today's standards go, it was a plain hug, but it was enough to be exciting.

It was a time of enchantment when we believed almost any dream would come true before long. Future success or failure never entered our minds. Money was unimportant. The well-to-do teenagers had their weekly allowances (mine went from twenty-five to fifty cents somewhere along the line). Boys whose families were poor worked at odd jobs. Girls did baby-sitting, though it wasn't called that then, or helped with ironing.

We had no idea of the world we were about to be involved with. To us a war was fought because Paul Revere had something to do with hanging one or two lanterns from a bell tower, or because Lincoln had to unify the nation.

Furthermore, a depression was a hole in the ground. The mental kind was described as follows: "She isn't feeling quite herself" or "She suffers from sick headaches." The weaker sex was allowed to have the vapors but men were supposed to be impervious.

Once when a desperate husband tried to kill his wife, Father said, "Something must have been the matter with him."

Whatever tragedies occurred were not broadcast by the media, for there were no radio news bulletins, no television reports. The *Post Crescent* went so far as to announce fires of "undetermined origin" but I doubt whether Lizzie Borden would have had a front-page spread.

Sometimes when I came in from skating with a few friends and Mama's Clio Club was meeting, the women's voices would suddenly lower as we sat in the kitchen drinking hot chocolate floating with marshmallows, but we would pay no attention. (Hot chocolate was made by shaving slivers of rich dark German chocolate bars. No mixes.)

Our own dramas occurred when two best friends stopped speaking to one another or when a member of the football team fell from a ladder while he was helping his father reroof the house or when some unfortunate friend was under house arrest by irate parents because of a terrible grade in English Composition!

Sometimes I did not even keep up with school problems, for young love came into my life early in my freshman year, with trumpets blowing, banners flying, silver lances shining. It really is not a subject for prose at all, but deserves poetry. I began to write verse at once, secretly at night, after my parents had gone to bed and my bedroom door was closed. This bothered Timmie since no Irish likes shut doors, but he put up with it by stretching out on my bed with his mahogany ears spread full sail on my pillow.

I already at that time had a best friend named Peggy. She was tall, leggy, long-necked. She walked with an odd rolling gait. She had dark hair, always windblown, dark eyes and a narrow, smiling mouth. Most of the time she wore a full bright blue coat that flapped around her knees. Her personality was quick, vibrant, witty and intelligent. She lived on the west side of town near the cemetery, so every funeral procession went by her front door.

Perhaps this was why we talked so much about life and death and the future, as well as ourselves (always a fascinating subject). We both read as if there were no tomorrow. After

school I walked her home, then she walked me home, then
I walked her home, usually getting home myself five minutes
before Father. If I was later than he, Mama had a hard
time.

"Where's Gladys?"

"She'll be home soon."

"What is she doing?"

"Just out walking with Peggy."

"She's had plenty of time to get home. This walking
around has got to stop."

Both Peggy and I (before I fell in love) took boys casually, probably because there was no shortage of them. As
we saw it, their function in life was to provide us with escorts
for dances, picnics and occasional movies and to be our
partners in tennis, skating, boating on the river, croquet.
Peggy did not really care for sports since she was awkward,
always dropping tennis balls, tripping over wickets, driving
croquet balls through kitchen windows.

Today she would be on a glossy magazine cover, shown
leaning against a boat rail with those long, elegant legs clad
in flared flame-colored pants, a sleeveless blouse open at the
neck. Exotic necklaces would suit the long neck. Her hair
might be plastered to her narrow head. But I imagine that
while she was posing for the photographer she would at some
moment fall in the water.

In that era the pencil-thin figure caused no stir. She was
just another girl, gay, amusing, outspoken, but certainly no
sex symbol. Neither was I. When we walked those endless
miles together I had to look up to see her face or be satisfied
just to stare at her shoulder bones. Like all the Bagg family,
I was short, which meant I was to spend most of my life
finding that things were out of reach. My neck was short

and the muscles ached a good deal as I tried to peer over things. I was thin and agile but later would be stocky as a Bagg must be. My hair was light and naturally curly but too fine to be practical. My eyes were blue, and that was about all. My energy was enough to wear most friends out. I always seemed to be running after something, even when there was nothing to run after.

I found life on the whole very satisfying until the day I looked up from my seat in assembly room and saw one particular boy coming down the aisle. He moved lightly; he was tall but there was a compactness about his body. He was as erect as if a steel rod ran through his spine (most of us tended to slouch a bit). It was midday and the sun came through the big windows, making his blond hair a halo above the sea-blue eyes and straight mouth.

Just where and when lightning strikes can never be predicted, avoided, or invited. But in that musty, crowded room, on a warm spring day, from an absolutely cloudless sky, the bolt exploded on one target, namely me. He happened to glance aside and saw my face, and I am thankful my expression was not recorded for history. I have never been any good at dissembling although I have worked hard at it at times.

He grinned.

The rest of that day is a blur. Even the endless walking with Peggy did not calm me down, and I seem to remember Mama taking my temperature when I wandered in that night. At midnight I was still writing poems full of Greek gods, and by morning I began to think about suicide. The other side of that coin of young love is a grinding anguish with which I was to become intimate. But when I met Jan for the first time, my reaction was acutely feverish. Mama figured I was coming down with something and was tempted to keep me at home that morning. At the suggestion, I roused myself enough to stage a real tantrum. Father poked around in the medicine cabinet and gave me a couple of pills which upset my stomach. My school record that day could have been bettered by a moron.

But after school he was on the steps talking to a couple of other boys, and he happened to come over and speak to me.

Peggy walked home alone.

Peggy's and my friendship was not damaged, which made her a model for that whole estate. That spring and thereafter she bore with the fact that I had only one subject on my mind. I could no longer pay any attention to reincarnation, or ghosts, or whether prehistoric man was ever happy. All I wanted to talk about was *him*. If he went to football practice after school, we walked as always back and forth, but if he stood waiting on the school steps, Peggy went on by herself.

As usual, I was in trouble with Father. He did not want this boy hanging around the house. Mama did her best, even going so far as to conceal the fact that what was wrong with the big clock was that I kept setting it back an hour so it would seem as if I were coming home on time. Mama's warm, loving heart accepted my new friend easily, and he responded eagerly. His own father and mother were dead and he lived with an aunt and uncle, and Mama was born to mother anyone who needed it.

My first attack of jealousy arose because I accused him of coming home with me just to see Mama! He loved to sit in the kitchen and talk to her when I wanted to be out walking with him in our own mysterious world.

If only I could have understood my father. It is a pity

that we seldom do understand a person at the time when it is vital, and the understanding often comes too late. Now I know how difficult it was for him to feel me pull away and become a separate person. Having lost two children, he now felt he was losing a third, but in a way more definite than death itself. He wanted to continue to be the center of my universe as he had always been. Moreover, he had built this elegant house and expected both Mama and me to be in it whenever he was at home.

In the past whenever Father decided to tramp around in cornfields outside town to hunt for Indian relics, I went hopping along beside him. If he felt like fishing, I went fishing. I left my line in long enough for a fish to bite but Father never did, as no fish could find his line quickly enough for him. If he felt like showing off his ability as a marksman, I watched as he hit the bull's-eye. We also spent hours in his darkroom in Science Hall while he taught me to develop and print photographs of glacial moraines, white birch stands, sunsets, fossils and rocks.

When my weekly piano lessons gave me enough ability to play a few songs, I played while he sang. He even wrestled with the problem of teaching me chess, at which, of course, he was expert.

But from the time I met Jan I was always somewhere else, supposedly practicing for my part in the school play or working on the school *Clarion* or studying at someone's house but actually off with my love. Occasionally Jan could use his ancient family car but not often. Mostly we played tennis or walked around. He had two small black cocker spaniels that were with us a good deal. We went to Peggy's house with a few classmates fairly often. Her mother never noticed who came, or when.

We stayed at my house when Father was at the college

for faculty meetings or whatever. But as I think back on that period, I wonder how many hundreds of miles we just walked. My Bagg feet suffered. The arches would ache so much that I used to step on stones to press the arches up. I looked for stones to step on whenever we were not on pavement. My tireless companion never noticed. He swung along with his easy gait, always half a step ahead and never out of breath. In summer I suffered from the heat; he never felt it. In winter I was numb with cold; he was comfortable. All I can say is that I never complained. I would have been happy to walk around hell or freeze to death in the Arctic, provided he was there.

Young love provides a special kind of insulation. But it never insulates from anguish. Jan often went off to the north woods to a place where there were jobs cutting timber. He always went at the wrong time but any time was wrong as far as I was concerned. He was gone one whole spring vacation and I barely survived.

It was small comfort that he sent me the first flowers of the spring with his love. They were a shoeboxful of arbutus he had picked himself (this was before conservation prohibited picking arbutus). The tiny, waxen, pinky blossoms and polished leaves glowed in a bed of wet cotton. The delicate fragrance was cool and fresh. All the corsages and occasional orchids that later came into my life only made me remember that box of arbutus. Flowers fade but memories have their own life. I saved the desiccated bouquet until it became a dead brown powder.

When he was gone I wrote reams of poems which nobody ever saw, but I did keep up with my homework purely out of fear of my father. (My eventual graduation with honors was something Father accomplished just by being the man he was.)

Our dreams were childish and simple, for we lived in a simple world. Jan would work his way through college and then we would get married and live happily ever after. Father would get used to the idea. I went so far as to learn a little rudimentary cooking from my gifted mother, although up to that time I had only eaten with great relish her gourmet meals. Aside from washing the dishes and keeping my room clean, I had been exempt from housework so I could study more.

If I had to cook a meal for Father when Mama was at a church affair, I made bacon and eggs and the bacon never would lie down and behave. Part was burned, part still greasy. I could do shrimp wiggle and Welsh rarebit, but Father wasn't too crazy about either. Now I began to hover over my poor mother in the kitchen, asking questions, which later paid off. She died before I wrote the first of five cookbooks and I am sorry she never saw them.

Lovemaking in that time was something that the youngsters of today could never envision. Girls were to stay "pure" until the wedding vows were taken. Young ladies never entertained young men alone in apartments or off in the woods under a comfortable tree. If Jan had not followed the rules, I do not know what might have happened. As it was, we held hands and kissed each other with more passion than most of our group. I was satisfied if I could touch his hand as we went walking. Sex was a word never mentioned, much less written about in books and magazines. Any girl who "went too far" was a fallen woman at once. Love, for us, was based on more than sheer physical attachment, which may have been a good idea. Young people really knew more about each other as persons than I think they do nowadays.

Jan and I knew exactly what we were like as people, quite aside from our emotional involvement. We shared our lonely childhoods, the death of his parents, our ambitions, our innermost thoughts. I learned to appreciate his dry humor and practical outlook on life. He put up with my romantic overreacting to anything and everything. He was far more mature than I but tolerant of my childishness.

When I exploded about my father, his comment was, "If your father could love people as he loves rocks, things would be different."

I remember March 10 of my junior year, in spite of my inability to recall dates. March in Wisconsin is wild and windy, often with hills white with new snow. Unexpectedly, a few days of false spring arrive, inspiring housewives to prop open storm doors and fill houses with bright, clean air. Hardy or reckless souls hang out a few blankets and talk about spring housecleaning. The spring-cleaning urge, I think, is as much a part of nature's rhythm as the birds coming back and crocus blooming.

This March 10 the varnished lilac buds were swelling as we took the path downriver. The sweet rich smell of thawed earth warmed us. A couple of early redwings sang "Okalee" in the thickets.

The old man was there outside the boathouse, puttering around.

"Guess I could let you have a canoe," he said. "Kind of early, aren't you? Better watch the current."

The canoe was flaky with red paint, the paddles chipped, but she floated. I paddled in front. We did not talk until we were well out on the deep river. For one thing, when you go canoeing you do not face each other and talking is easier when you can at least get a sidelong glance.

The sound of the dam down below was loud since the river was sweeping the snowmelt over it. The dam was one reason I was forbidden to go canoeing there, but I never gave it a thought. The few unfortunate boaters who were swept over just did not know much, in my opinion.

I seldom sang out loud since I could not carry a tune, but I hummed, "We were sailing along on Moonlight Bay."

My happiness was as wide and deep as the river rolling along beneath us. What more could a girl ask than to be in a canoe with her idol? I even forgot to be terrified at what Father would do if he found out. Someone has said eternity can be in a moment. So it was.

When the sun moved over the wooded shore, we turned back and paid the man—I think a whole quarter. As we climbed the steep path, Jan stopped in a patch of sun and leaned against a pine tree while I caught up.

"I have to tell you something," he said.

"What is it?"

"I don't know how to say it, but I have been having a very bad dream. I can't get it out of my head."

"I have bad dreams sometimes, too."

"But this seems so real I can't put it away."

"Tell me."

"You'll think I am silly, but I keep dreaming about war."

I leaned against him. "That's nothing to worry about," I said. The war that had begun in Europe was not anything that concerned our young lives. It was remote and unreal.

"Yeah, I know it. But the thing is, I seem to be in it." His face was troubled. "Why should I have such a crazy dream?"

"Nobody knows anything about dreams," I said.

"Maybe I won't have it anymore now that I have told you."

"No. I guess you can forget it."

Then we addressed ourselves to a real worry, that of getting me home before Father came from college.

I was to think of that March day a good many times in the next few years, but he never once referred to his dream again. I never asked about it because a vague fear kept me silent. We had not heard about precognition and perhaps it *was* only a bad dream.

It was a gay spring, a hot summer and a golden autumn. Most days were clear except for the final Saturday of the football season. The sky split in two to let the floods descend. The football field was deep with black mud. The boys looked small crouched in the curtain of rain. The opposing team—Oshkosh, I think—seemed gigantic. In those days the conflict was chiefly body against body, minus the protective padding and insulation of today. Two of our boys were laid out in the first quarter and carried off.

The spectators sat on the open bleachers. The boards were warped so we sat in pools of water. Mama had made me bundle up but this meant my wraps soaked up more water. There was no half-time jumping around. Some people went home. The visiting team was ahead by three points.

The third quarter we played against the rising wind. Neither team scored. Our two field-goal attempts went down the drain, as did a long forward pass which might have saved the day.

"Maybe we ought to start home," said Peggy, making a swishing sound as she squirmed around.

"Go if you want to. I won't desert our team." I was noble.

It was growing dark (no field lights, of course) when the

storybook ending came in the fourth quarter. Jan, who played left end, sloshed into a long end run and a touchdown.

For a moment, winning the game stunned us all. The teams began to straggle along the field. Then one bedraggled girl jumped from the bleachers and flew past the coaches and umpires, hair streaming, wraps flopping, one rubber missing. She flung herself at the left end and hugged him right there on the field, in public! This unbecoming behavior made the boys laugh.

It also meant that I was plastered with mud from one filthy football suit. Explaining my condition to Father came later, but at the moment it didn't matter. We walked off the field together (no dugouts or locker rooms then).

When Jan tried to wipe the mud from his face, he only smeared it. His hair was wet and black instead of gold. But when he got his breath, the old familiar grin lit his face.

"Awful mess," he commented. "You're a mess, too."

I was to spend many days broiling or freezing at football games, even sitting through a blizzard at Ann Arbor once. The great days of the Green Bay Packers with Lombardi kept one addict happy. I even wrote a football story once that was printed in a booklet for the armed forces (in case they had time to read, which is doubtful). It was based on the old mousetrap play and was the only story included in that booklet by a woman writer. I was prouder of that than of my first hardcover book.

Since I do not believe in any violence, there is no sense in this at all, for football is what they call a contact sport and the contact breaks a lot of bones. I should be crusading against it, but instead I am glued to the television set for all the big games. It proves nobody can be consistent all the time!

I suppose it all goes back to that eventful Saturday and to that one touchdown.

Our senior year had a strangeness about it. By then, events in the outside world had begun to invade our peaceful town, and a cloud of anxiety took some of the color from the sky. Adults worried about what might happen. Nobody took polls in those days to find out whether the town voted to leave Europe to its own business and stay on our own soil or go over and settle everything.

Practically all the boys in the senior class belonged to a reserve group, with tan uniforms and boots. I cannot recall the exact title but I know we all felt it was rather like an extension of Boy Scouts. They did some drilling and marching but I never knew what else.

My own war with Father took up too much time. The issue was college. I was not to go to Lawrence but back to Massachusetts (where else?), and he chose Wellesley as most suitable. I cried enough to water a desert. I stopped speaking to him. I pulled all the stops, in short. All I wanted was to stay home with Mama, Timmie and, yes, with Father, and to take all the courses Jan would be taking at Lawrence. We would have four years with perhaps a bit more freedom than in high school. After we graduated, there would be some version of that little grey home in the west.

"What would we live on?" asked my realistic Jan. "I have to figure on working my way through college. My aunt and uncle have done all they can for me."

Figuring out money matters was not my dish. Father did not let me even supplement my allowance by baby-sitting (we called it "staying at the Jones's house while the parents went out").

Spring of our senior year was the loveliest ever. Lilacs

were a deeper amethyst than usual and their pointed dark leaves a polished green. Violets blossomed everywhere. Householders who rose on dewy mornings to mow the lawn without waiting for the grass to dry out clogged their lawn-mowers with violets. Over all, maples and elms filtered the sun through green canopies.

My lasting recollection of the small town was of a green world, for the ax of progress had not yet cut down the trees to widen streets, build more buildings and make paved lots for parking as automobiles took over the economy. The street-car ran on the same tracks down the length of Main Street. The railroad station still had a few hitching posts near the platform, but beyond the unloading area for freight cars there were the trees.

Outside town, the farmlands laid emerald carpets, which would change to pale gold in haying time. Cornfields were green, too, tasseled with silk. And the woodlands were al-most a black-green where the pines stood. The white birches were lighter green and their trunks silvery. Most of them were to go, not because of bulldozers and men clearing the land but because peeling off birch bark became the rage. In early summer people could buy toy birch-bark canoes, boxes covered with bark, booklets bound in it.

Roses came early that June, red, white, pink and my favorite yellow tea roses with spiny stems. I do not remember one house that lacked enough roses to fill the air with cool, spicy scent and dazzle the eyes with luminous colors.

And so we came to graduation day.

After looking forward to graduation for four years, we did not want it. We wanted to walk up the steps to the old building in the morning carrying our books, to worry about the next exam, plan the next class party. We wanted to be

a class, a familiar, integrated group. We didn't, in fact, want
change.

There was also a sense that the world was not the planet
we were born on. The future was a dark void. Insulated as
we were in our small midwestern town, we knew an era was
ending. The quiet air had echoes of guns firing. Somehow
we sensed we were the last generation to finish four years of
high school in a stable America.

However, graduation itself was as usual. Scrubbed and
smelling of Ivory soap, dressed in rented or borrowed robes,
we marched across the rostrum. Not one boy had long hair
or a mustache, much less a beard. No girl had a flow of hair
down to her stomach. There were no false eyelashes or
smudges of eye shadow.

The class president, Bill Helms, gave the main address.
He was a big, gentle boy with neat, wheat-colored hair, a
square, rosy face and grey-blue eyes. He was more mature
than the rest of us, and his speech was simple, direct, full of
feeling. He was Jan's best friend and Jan was immensely
proud of him.

Afterward we were gay and laughed a lot, waving our
blue-ribboned diplomas, accepting congratulations, making
dates for the summer picnics. When the festivities were over
we scattered like birds. Most of the boys had lined up summer jobs. Most of the girls were getting ready for college,
and summer meant organizing the right clothes for September. The moon shone on the Fox River; the stars were in
their accustomed places. The night air smelled of sulfur and
roses and newly cut grass.

History caught us unawares. Not long after graduation,
the day came when the train pulled into the dusty, sooty

station to carry the boys away. Those who had been in the high school reserve were to continue their military training in the army—again, like the Boy Scouts, to "be prepared." Most of the townspeople were on the platform. The day coaches were packed. The boys managed to get the windows up so they could lean out and wave. Jan and Bill had their heads close together at one window.

Some mothers cried but most stood silent, just looking. Fathers could have been carved from granite. Small children sped like waterbugs in and out. Smoke from the engine curled up to a blue, serene sky. When the engine began to struggle for breath and move slowly down the track, a few of us girls ran along beside the train until it gathered speed.

The outstretched arms of the boys kept waving. They gave the scene a frightening look, as if the passengers were begging for release

"We'll be back soon!"

"I'll write."

The last image I had was of Jan and Bill framed in one filthy window, smiling, sweating, reaching out.

They were to be moved from one training camp to another, never knowing the next stop. More than a year later they were to be shipped across the ocean as part of the Rainbow Division.

Soon after that, Bill's head was blown off as he stood next to Jan in a trench. He was the first of our friends to die.

Breezes from Waban Blow Gently

IT SEEMS STRANGE to me now that we all went ahead with our lives that September as if nothing could touch us. College was a world unto itself, and most of the time I was totally immersed despite the events that were taking place outside that small world and despite my longing for Jan.

Wellesley freshmen in the autumn of 1916, when I first got there, were housed in an old frame building in the village outside campus. It must have once been an elegant private mansion or possibly an inn. It was tall and lank and dark brown. I remember it as dark brown and dark green inside, too. The housemother, Miss Rusk, seemed dark brown also.

Miss Rusk was tall and thin, with dark brown hair and

75

dark brown eyes. As she came down a narrow hall, her brown suit would blend into the walls in a strange way (I could have imagined this). There was, to me, nothing motherly about her; she frightened me. Now that I am presumably wiser, I appreciate the impossible job she had. Coping with too many homesick girls jammed into ugly, small rooms was problem enough. A room barely large enough for one had two, and roommates moved in ready to battle for drawer space and for the small table desk near the window.

Noanett was supposed to be temporary housing until an extra freshman dormitory was built on campus, but that year money was not even available to remodel the old dormitory, not even to change the brown burlap halfway up the walls.

I was a complete misfit. My clothes were fine back in a small town in the Midwest but a disaster here in the East. The other girls, who later became cherished friends, seemed sophisticated and elegant. I was too timid to recite in class, and the required math course paralyzed me. The only comfort I had was the glossy of Theda Bara pinned on the burlap above my narrow bed.

Before long, I got sick. Miss Rusk came in and felt my forehead. She smelled of starch and cologne. In a few minutes she rustled away and called the college doctor.

Dr. Raymond was brisk, efficient and immaculate in her white garb. She took time to look me over and ask me a few questions, the main one being how many times I had been away from home. Her diagnosis was brief and positive. She wrote *homesickness* on her pad and said I would feel better soon. I was to take aspirin (which always upset my stomach). Somehow I did feel better in a day or so, chiefly because she had treated me like a person.

I had a couple of tray meals which were better than the regular food, and a couple of girls dropped in. Peg Hornbrook and Jo Clark were close friends from then on, and still are, and I met Molly Morris, who moved in that first year to room with me.

By the time I got over being frightened if an autumn leaf fell on me as I walked across campus, I had discovered Elizabeth Mainwaring and Katharine Lee Bates. Miss Mainwaring presided over English Composition; Katharine Lee Bates made the world of Shakespeare precious to me.

They were so different, and supremely gifted. Miss Mainwaring was a firm, shapely woman with shining brown hair and piercing dark eyes. She wore elegant shirtwaists over a full bosom, and the frills at her wrists set off hands any artist would have wanted to paint. Her suit skirts fitted snugly over definite hips.

Miss Bates was plump as a ripe apple and did not look academic at all. She looked as if she should be rolling pie dough in a country kitchen. In her spare time she wrote things like "America the Beautiful" and became nationally famous. The students she taught realized only that they counted the hours between classes.

The effect a superb teacher has can never be measured. These two were to influence me all the rest of my life, giving direction and focus I had never had. I spent much of my four years trying to skip required courses in order to take more of theirs. I could not change the rigid college curriculum, but I did manage to become a friend of Miss Mainwaring's and spend some time with her, even being invited to lunch while she talked about writing. She made things like "Eggs Caracas," and I always ate like a starving orphan even while I was walking on clouds.

In that era one took what the college decided, a varied curriculum. I was not allowed to take German, which I loved, or more Latin. I had to take French, botany, geology (shades

of Father), the inevitable math (which erased my chance
for Phi Beta Kappa at once). But when I discuss educational
programs, I have two opposite points of view (it seems to
be a habit of mine).

Is it better to have free choice for students so they can
study only what they are interested in and thus learn more
in special fields, or is it better that they learn something in
as many areas as possible so their horizons are widened as
they go out into life?

I could have acquired much more in literature and composition (or creative writing) but for two courses that were
required for graduation, Bible History and Art 13.

Seal Thompson taught Bible. She was small, wiry, red-
headed. Her mind was lightning-fast, her wit like a drawn
lance. She always skipped down the corridor to class and
opened with a prayer. I began her course as receptive as a
stone wall, for I had been raised with more familiarity with
the Bible than I wanted. The church left few pages unturned
except for some of the songs of Solomon which I had read
on my own.

However, before long I felt Bible should be required of
every student. It became the most exciting and fascinating
study. It came alive. The history of the early peoples had
the charm of archaeological findings. The depth and beauty
of the Old and New Testaments lit up our ignorant minds.
There was never a boring moment, and often some of us sat
up after hours, dunking marshmallows in our pale cocoa and
arguing about it.

Art 13 was required of any student who had not taken
any art courses. It was scheduled for senior year when all I
wanted was one more year with Miss Mainwaring. I admit it
could have been dull, but Myrtilla Avery was the professor.
Years later when I first saw El Greco's *View of Toledo,* my

favorite painting, I remembered Miss Avery and wished I could thank her for bringing an appreciation of great art into my life.

Life, I now believe, needs as many open doors as possible. I am grateful to my alma mater for making me open some doors I would have avoided if the regime had been less rigid.

In fact, my whole philosophy is built on a belief that the more we can appreciate, the richer we are. Most of us would walk past any closed door on our way to the familiar open one we already love. So, thank you, Seal Thompson and Myrtilla Avery, and also Wellesley College, which insisted that more doors be opened.

As a side comment, I feel Latin ought to be required from high school right on through. This would horrify my young friends who don't want to be bored with any old deceased language. But since the roots of so many of our English words are Latin, it is often possible to understand a strange word quite easily because the Latin root is dreaming inside it! My four years of Latin in high school were not enough but have been a help all my life.

One of my dearest friends, Helen Eliot, is a physics teacher, and she feels I should have had physics since it is so basic. Perhaps if I had been forced to take it, I might understand how electricity gets into the light bulb, although this is problematical. Every time I turn on a lamp I wonder why it begins to glow. So physics also should be required, even if one fails, as I surely would have.

I had enough trouble with required botany, but later on I longed to know more about it. My main memory of that course was a field trip for identifying plants, and it was completely lost on me. It was the only time in my career I cheated. One discouraged little plant was a mystery to me until my companion bent down and twiddled the leaves so they looked like dog ears and I knew it was dogbane! It took years of country living in later life for me really to learn something about trees, plants, flowers and bushes.

College life at that time dated back to the Victorian era. I cannot even describe it to my young college friends of today, for they think I am indulging in fiction. We were allowed to go to Boston for matinee performances of the Symphony and to the art museum and occasionally to the Arboretum when lilacs bloomed. We took the train in and out, always with someone.

We were not permitted to ride in an automobile on Sunday, and I remember watching one of my friends running along beside her family's car when her parents came to visit her. She could *not* get in that car.

In the daytime we could walk outside campus, even as far as Natick. We could go canoeing on Lake Waban, which abutted the campus. We could go to the village tearoom and to the Inn on weekends, but not at night.

We could entertain boys on weekends in the safety of the dormitory parlors, but no male ever set foot in any other part of the building. Naturally there were no recreation rooms or smoking rooms. One brilliant girl was expelled during her senior year for smoking a single cigarette, which some misguided beau had brought along when he came to call.

We signed slips when we went out and slips when we came in. No private life was possible at any time.

Usually a housemother was around when we did entertain on Sunday afternoons, so personal conversations were at a minimum. Tea and cookies provided refreshments for those hardy males who came. It was chiefly a world of women.

Even this hangover from the past had some advantages, for it meant we formed close, enduring friendships with our own sex, which may not be as usual in colleges today.

There was no rebellion against the rules for we came from families which had much the same pattern. However, we managed sometimes to overstep them. For instance, in my sophomore year I slipped off to Boston on the pretense of going to the art museum when Jan came there on his last leave before being shipped overseas. (Boston was the point of departure for a good many of the troops.)

Jan and I ate at Durgin Park and walked around Boston and bought pickled limes (famous because of Amy in *Little Women*). We wandered in the old cemetery by Trinity Church and looked at the grave of my Hatch ancestor. Then we said good-bye in Old South Station. He bought me yellow roses and, as we parted, one rose fell between us in the grime of the station.

He almost missed reporting to the ship, and his officer went into a typical military rage.

"But I told him I was saying good-bye to my girl," wrote Jan, "and then he said it was all right."

My friends and I closed ranks to protect each other. We never told anyone if one of us missed the required train back; and if our faces were swollen from weeping, we explained that a cold was coming on. So far as I know, no one was ever caught, but now I wonder whether a few housemothers weren't wise to it all and said nothing. There was, after all, a war on—for the United States had finally gotten into it—and perhaps they were inclined to be lenient.

And the war was always there, dense and shapeless as a fog. We did not talk of it. We watched the mail. When the first death that affected one of us was reported, we acted from instinct and kept quiet. The girl was actually engaged, with the permission of her parents, and she and her fiancé planned a big wedding as soon as they graduated from college. The whole wall of her room was filled with photographs of him. Then came the telegram—and the mere arrival of a telegram was something special at that time.

We were all too young to be accustomed to death. We were learning, and this particular portion of our education was nothing we could study in a book and pass exams on. It did knit us together in a way nothing else could, but we did not appreciate the experience. Some of us already had cedar hope chests with embroidered linens laid in with lavender, along with silver bowls and initialed silverware.

I do not think any of us had a real knowledge of the World War. There were no able news commentators, no panel discussions. There was no television. We did have complete faith in our government, which seems hard to imagine nowadays, and we had no doubt about winning the war. Meanwhile we walked with terror. When the newspapers reported light casualties, this was small comfort, for just one casualty could affect our whole life. Governments operate on figures; we operated as individuals.

I, at least, did not know enough geography to identify the places where the worst battles were fought. Marne, Saint-Mihiel, Argonne—these were names picked from nightmares.

We could only watch for the mail in those slivers of envelopes. And rather hopelessly send parcels, most of which never arrived. We made Red Cross bandages and knitted sweaters. My one attempt at a sweater was a failure because one sleeve seemed to shoot off from the neck and one was around the hips. A more gifted friend ripped it out and knitted it over. I did manage several grey scarves, which may have been passed out to children in villages destroyed by the armies. Or they may have ended at the bottom of the sea, where presumably the deep-sea creatures never wore them.

We lived on two levels in a curious way, as I suppose all women do in war. One level, the dense fog of the war, was always there. On the other level we tried to acquire an education, make friends, save up enough money for dinner at the Inn, topped off with fudge cake.

Sophomore year I was fortunate enough to move to Tower Court. My roommate and I had a big room, two desks, closet space for two, wide windows looking toward Lake Waban, a kitchenette down the corridor and our best friends on the same floor. Tower Court seemed like a palace, but better heated. The spacious living room downstairs was what I think would be called Tudor, and there were sofas, easy chairs and real rugs. It was so elegant we felt timid about using it when relatives came to visit.

My roommate that second year was to become a major influence in my life. Jill and I had met when we were fourteen, when her parents sent her to an informal camp on Lake Winnebago. The parents of two of my friends ran it. It consisted of a precariously put together summer cottage on the lake shore. It was, to say the least, casual. I remember even the teakettle leaked. It was feverishly hot in summer, well furnished with mosquitoes and smelled of algae. But everybody was happy, and I spent many days there as a nonpaying guest. When I found out Jill was also destined for Wellesley, we had an instant bond, for she did not want to go either.

A nearly fatal scarlet fever kept her from entering college till a year after I began, but when she did come, we unpacked our impedimenta in Tower Court.

Reality is a concept most difficult to define. Part of ourselves always enters into our judgment to color it. I do not believe an impersonal estimate of anything or anyone is possible. I may go further and say if we realized this, there would be fewer bitter arguments. Therefore, my analysis of Jill is shaped by my own self, and although I loved her more as the years went on, I would be the last to say I could accurately describe the reality of her.

Perhaps what makes friendship and love exciting is the continuing discovery of another personality. There is always a sense of wonder about it. I feel this also in nature, for no rose is exactly like another rose, no sunsets are the same, no birdsong duplicates another. Life is a process of discovery, of new perceptions.

The Jill who was my roommate did not seem at first complex. She was another midwestern girl, raised in the corn belt in Illinois in a town similar to mine except there was no college to color the atmosphere. Her father's family originally came from Scotland, sturdy, quiet, big-boned, deeply religious in the most orthodox sense. The Presbyterian faith answered all spiritual needs. Her father was half owner of the town's prosperous lumber business, and years later, when he lived with me for a time, I could not find him interested in any of what we then called cultural matters. He was a good man but almost as stern a disciplinarian as my own father. His one outside interest was golf—perhaps the Scottish heritage—which he played with grim intensity.

Jill's mother was somehow descended from the Edgar Allan Poe family. She was a small, quick woman, dark-haired, as lively in conversation as her husband was slow. When they dressed for church, she looked fragile in frilly clothes. He towered over her like a mountain, erect and moving deliberately.

I wish I could have known Jill's mother well for she was an exciting person, but when I visited them she was involved in so many activities, especially the DAR, that she seldom had time to sit around. Indeed, I think of her as too volatile and restless ever to enjoy the wicker rocking chair on the front porch.

Their house was typical of that period, gingerbread trimmings and a peaked gable. The furniture was comfortable but not elegant. Jill was proud of owning a bird's-eye maple bedroom set for her room.

Jill's sister was blond, blue-eyed, built like her mother and endowed with such feminine charm that the boys who flocked around never realized she had a mind so brilliant it would have frightened them. I knew it the first time I stayed there and was in awe of her. She had her mother's flair for clothes, on top of everything else, which made me feel dumpy and shabby. I was told she had been delicate as a child, but the fragility was deceptive. When she got to college, she graduated in three years, which was a rarity at that time. She was two years younger than Jill, so our paths seldom crossed during college.

Jill had her father's big, sturdy frame and the grey-blue eyes, but she had her mother's night-dark hair, which she never could "do anything with." She settled for what we called a Dutch cut, just a cap covering her beautifully shaped head. She had a loose, easy walk like a farmer, and when we went anywhere, I brought up the rear, panting. I always saw more of her back than anything else.

This much about Jill and her family was fact, but reality lay deeper. As I grew intimate with them over the years, I sensed a quiet strength in her father, reminding me of the early farmers who battled the midwestern wilderness and wrenched a living from it for their families. Under his stubborn, impassive exterior was faith in a God who blessed you if you "did right" and who always punished sin. The one thing he and my volatile, passionate father had in common was that their God did not specialize in forgiveness. Jill and I were raised in the belief that if we did not obey God in all ways, we would be punished.

Her mother, I later thought, compensated as well as possible for an unromantic Victorian marriage by pouring her energies into whatever was allowable—church, DAR, civic work, women's groups. She spent herself lavishly, but I do not believe she was fulfilled. Today she would have been a career woman and a smashing one.

Jill's sister managed, as she grew up, to retain the image of the gentle, utterly feminine woman while quietly succeeding in a competitive man's world. Her wit and charm only increased; her seductively soft voice and gentle manners kept her brilliant mind from being a handicap in her personal relationships.

Jill seemed a complete opposite. I got used to hearing, "I can't believe they are sisters! They are so different!"

It did appear so. Built like her father, Jill was also a golf enthusiast. Scarlet fever had left a damaged heart that kept her from violent sports, but she was a champion golfer as far as skill went, and her father was proud of the silver trophies she had won so easily.

She "took golf" at college, but a fatal weakness developed rapidly. She had absolutely no competitive spirit and never had that passion to win that is the mark of the true champion. It was my task to toil around the golf course behind her, carrying her golf bag and trying to learn which club was which. My frustration at never being at the top in any sport was greatly eased just by watching her roll that silly little ball into the cup with an easy swing. Our first real battle was when she decided to give up golf entirely because she did not want to waste her time!

I then learned something useful to me the rest of our time together. Once she made up her mind, Jill was unshakable. She usually would not even argue.

"You're just a stubborn Scot," I said.

"I am not really Scotch, just on Papa's side," she said.

"But don't you want to be a real champion?"

"No," she said.

I was reminded of this years later when I had a talk with her husband in the days when they played bridge. He was a winner in anything he took up, which made him an outstanding surgeon, among other things.

"She could be a good bridge player," he told me, "but she just doesn't give a darn about winning."

I felt a surge of sympathy for him. "She never will," I said.

But there was a curious thing in her complex personality. She never cared about being at the top of the class, but she always wanted to be an A-plus student in any course.

I now believe that she did not care about anything except satisfying something deep within herself, and what went on outside her inner consciousness was shadowy, unreal. When she sat up all night trying to absorb some deep German book I could not fathom at all, she was following a personal dream.

This was not a trait in her we could ever discuss. She would only say, "I want to understand all of that psychology."

A basic temperament set her apart from the rest of our group. We were so curious about ourselves in that period. We could talk for hours about our feelings, ideas, hopes, ambitions. We called it discussing LIFE in capitals, but we were actually exploring our own personalities. Jill was not interested in studying herself. She was inhabiting herself without concern; that is the best way I can express it. This gave her a calmness and steadiness the rest of us lacked. When we chittered like house sparrows, she never interrupted us to talk about herself. When we argued fiercely about unimportant matters, she was quiet as a woodland pool.

Most women's voices tend to rise when they are in a group, often so much as to make my sensitive ears ache, like too much rock music. Her voice never rose. It was light, relatively uninflected, and she never spoke rapidly. I learned, in times of trouble, to find that voice a kind of security.

By senior year I had given up trying to be witty when we met at the end of the day. I worked hard at being amusing and could always make our friends laugh. I fancied myself as a comedian at that time. But my best efforts failed to make Jill laugh. She did not have a conventional sense of humor. Cartoons left her colder than a clam. Humorous writing that convulsed me never affected her at all. Nowadays when her two children and I are together regaling ourselves with funny stories, one of them will say, "Mother would never think this was funny." And when we laugh at the memory, there is a special cherishing in our voices.

But perhaps the worst problem I had during that time was that she never expressed her emotions. She would accept a peck on the cheek when we parted for vacations. I would run up and down the corridor, hugging and kissing everyone, misty-eyed. I would greet them on return with extravagant display.

Jill would stand on the station platform, composed, cool. "Good-bye. See you soon," she said. "I'll send a postcard."

I had to settle for that mild kiss, unreturned.

It embarrassed her to show any emotion, but it was not easy for me to accept this. In my family, emotions ran rampant, especially between Father and me. We always ended our bitter battles with his holding me (on his lap until I was in high school) and hugging and kissing and crying all at once.

Jill grew up in a regime where it was not proper to display feelings. Consequently, hers were deep as an underground river. It took time for me to realize the depth of them. Meanwhile I nursed hurt emotion as best I could.

Loving is, after all, an adventure into another personality. And love cannot survive once we give up exploring. When I discovered that Jill felt as much as I did but could never show it, we were both better off.

Love itself has as many meanings as an encyclopedia has definitions. This sweetest of four-letter words is to me life's greatest mystery. Friendship is only another facet of it. I do not use either carelessly. Sometimes I am accused of being too lavish with both, but I doubt whether there can be an oversupply. At least I never use up mine.

When I tell someone I love the dump man dearly, I mean it. I could write a book about this slight, weathered man with the dazzling smile and keen blue eyes who rides high in the monster bulldozer, waving at me to sit still until he comes to lug my trash for me. His philosophy would do credit to a savant. I am always cheered after a visit with him. And his sharp, salty wit brightens the darkest day.

My closest friends put up with being told how wonderful they are and so do the children and grandchildren, although some, I am sure, would prefer a more impersonal approach. I can't be cured! Jill soon grew used to my temperament, which was just as well since she was to be an integral part of my life as long as she lived. She never weakened enough to call me darling, or even dear, or any nickname. To the others in our group, I was Gladie (awful as it sounds) or G.L.B. or sweetie-pie and so on. I was Gladys to her.

I managed to persuade her to call our favorite friend from Wellesley, Josephine Clark, Jo, but never Jodie as I did. Terms of endearment always spilled over with me but never with Jill.

A name to her was a private identity not to be tampered with. With my usual inconsistency, I never liked my own name toyed with by strangers or by people I did not care for. But when anyone I have been fond of for some time finally stops calling me Mrs., I glow. After five years of friendship with one particular man, I went so far as to snap at him.

"I should think you might stop calling me Mrs. Taber by now."

"I was raised to call married ladies Mrs.," he said.

The next time we met, he conceded and said, "How are you, Gladys?"

When I sum up my thoughts about the world I inhabit, I think we would be better off if we expressed more warmth in our daily lives. I wonder whether the younger generation, with their love beads, love cults, chants and all the rest, may not be reacting to the reserve and stiffness of our own!

In any case, historians will have a field day analyzing what is wrong with our era, now that they have solved the Edwardian and Victorian periods. It is a pity we know so little about our own times.

This did not worry us while we were in college. We were entirely involved in day-by-day existence. We sang "Roses of Picardy" and "Over There" and "Back Home Again in Indiana"; we went to classes, drank gallons of hot cocoa, built up memories to carry with us.

We learned, among other things, what flu was like. The flu epidemic swept the campus like a hurricane. In Tower Court the attic was turned into an infirmary. We were hauled up there, dropped in cots, and lived or died according to our own constitutions.

The college did its best, but there were no flu inoculations at that time. Nobody, I think, even knew what flu was.

I was conscious enough to realize the imminence of death. Jill, in the next cot, never spoke. With her shaky heart and recurrent asthmatic attacks, she was an easy victim for the virus. Doctors dragged in and out, red-eyed. Nursing help was scarce. Food, by the time it reached the attic, was not tempting, but most of us couldn't eat anyway.

My blankets as well as sheets were soaked with sweat most of the time. Then they were like ice water as I went from fever to chills. When I had strength enough, I cried in the soaked pillow for my mother.

We were all too ill to notice when wrapped forms rolled by. No casualty list was ever published, then or later.

One day Mama spoke to my father.

"I feel something is wrong," she said. "Gladys is sick. I know it. I have packed a suitcase. Call up the station and find out about the next train to Chicago."

Fortunately, before she took that train, I passed the crisis. But anyone who disbelieves in ESP cannot argue with me because this epidemic was not publicized. The college did not want a panic, and what a disaster it would have been if all the parents had turned up in the village to be sheltered and fed and catch the virus themselves. Our college managed the catastrophe with incredible wisdom and strength.

The day came when Jill and I were back in our room and our immediate friends crawled down the corridor, one by one. The night sweats went on for some time, and we lived on toast and tea, but we were safe and out of the dark. The view of Waban looked like paradise. And we had dry sheets on our beds.

Two special memories float to the surface from this period. I would like to forget both.

The first is about the night I killed the mouse. Somehow a small mouse got into the kitchenette to enjoy the luxury of cheese and cracker crumbs. At a meeting in our room I was elected to dispatch him. The only two things that turned Jill to stone were mice and snakes. It seemed that Jo and Peg and the others felt the same way.

I explained I was no killer; I even stepped around ants to avoid them. Swatting the noisiest fly was left to Jill. I was, nevertheless, drafted in this crisis. I admitted I was not afraid of mice, and that left me defenseless.

Armed with one of Jill's golf clubs, I went to the kitchenette. He was a very small mouse, fawn-colored. He quivered as I advanced and swung the club (I think it was a putter). The next ten minutes we went around the small space like a pinwheel until finally he cowered under the counter in the farthest corner.

I killed him.

When I went back to the room, I hated everyone in it. I went to the bathroom, sick. I could not forget that tiny, soft body as it was crushed, nor how it felt, still warm, as I picked it up to put in the trash bin.

My friends admired me and assured me we would all have died from some mysterious disease carried by mice. I did not believe a word of it. I felt that if they could not share a few crumbs with a poor mite, they were never destined for heaven. Eventually I rejoined my part of the human race, but to this day I remember the horror.

My second recurring memory is of a different nature since it concerns simply my own survival. In my town we did not ski, but some of my friends had taken up skiing at college. One of them lent me her skis. She told me it was simple. All I had to do was stand on the top of the steep hill at Tower Court, jump off and soar to the bottom. That was the way to learn.

The bottom looked very far off as I stood teetering on the top that bitter, snowy day, but I braced myself and jumped off. It is possible my friend was really a deadly enemy; I shall never know. Wind and snow were my only companions as I did a crash landing at the bottom of the hill, miraculously avoiding a few pine trees.

Skis are not supposed to bend, but one ski seemed to be wrapped around my neck. When I got my head above the snowdrift, I found I was alive. I could even crawl on all fours.

I broke no bones, probably because the snow was soft and deep. But I bruise easily, and I went around for some time looking as if I had been dipped in purple dye. The only part of me that did not ache was my hair.

I never put on skis again. It was, no doubt, a good education, for I now watch champions skim the air, leaning forward over nothing, and I appreciate their skill. I now know you first ski on level snow until you learn something about the skis. And I know I was fortunate not to break my neck along with a few other bones!

Jill was away that day doing some kind of research in the Boston Library. She did not sympathize at all. She told me simply that I was a complete fool. I agreed thoroughly with her as I let the ice packs drip down my neck.

All during this period in our lives, we lived, as I have said, on two levels, in two worlds: the immediate world of classes and grades and college friendships and activities, and the other world of no-man's-land, terrible casualty counts and censored letters from Europe. Occasionally we had dates with young men not yet across the water. The dates were limited and formal, and my chief memory of them is eating fudge cake at the Inn. I was always hungry. And I always wished I were with Jan instead.

Roses Are Blooming in Picardy

MY PERSONAL RECORD of the war years consisted of a bundle of letters. The first ones, written from various training camps, were relatively long for a nonverbal eighteen-year-old. They were passionate and direct. They changed at the point when every letter had to be signed by a lieutenant who was censoring them. It was as if the censor leaned over Jan's shoulder as every word went down in that firm, slanted handwriting.

For months I kept the letters wrapped in waxed paper under my pillow, and since I was a restless sleeper, they usually were under the bed by morning. I spent a lot of time on my hands and knees fishing them out and wiping off the dust rolls.

I read them daily so the folds began to tear and the ink

to fade. The YMCA paper was not the best quality, nor was the ink. My answers must have been childish, unaware, but I wrote daily, or even twice a day, and my letters were long.

Mostly they were full of dreams and love, but completely without understanding of what we faced. My world still had that rose-colored future with a cottage smelling of lilacs and honeysuckle—with an occasional broiled steak. The sky was eternally blue, the sun golden, the moon at night a silver bowl, the heavens a garden of stars. It was forever summertime and it never rained (I do not like rain very much). I was never troubled by reality at that time.

And, at first, neither was Jan. The years of living that were to separate us were nothing but some blank pages to turn before we were together again. However, we did keep growing and in separate worlds.

The letters always began "Dearest Girl" partly because he knew how I hated my unromantic, pedestrian name. There were a few very early ones from Texas when the reserve corps was sent south, soon after leaving Appleton. These told about the heavy woolen suits he had to wear, the only kind the army afforded. His dream, Jan wrote, was to wear a nice cool summer suit and a silk shirt and a Panama hat and take me canoeing in the evening. He asked for a ribbon of mine to tie his identification tag around his neck.

He told me, too, that he always wanted to kiss me no matter where we were or who was around. The reason he hadn't kissed me for months was that he was afraid. This cleared up my doubts about how long it took him to fall in love when it took me one look!

The last letter from the South brought the news of his transfer to the Machine Gun Battery that would be leaving for France as soon as it was outfitted. His feelings were typical of the very young in those days. He said he was gladly

giving himself to our country because of what it had given
to us; it had protected us until we loved. If he did not come
back, he wrote, it would be a glorious sacrifice for both of
us! I should not be unhappy for I would know that I had
given our country the greatest gift I had, my love.

He meant to comfort me by adding that he would gladly
sacrifice his life to save me pain.

I cried all night suffering the most intense pain I ever
had known.

After the brief leave when we said good-bye, a few letters came, which were as difficult for me to read as for him
to have written. In one, dated October 3, 1917, he wrote
that he was reliving our last Sunday-morning walk. He reminded me how wonderfully pure and sweet the air had been
and how beautiful the colors. I agreed that the gods were
with us that morning. This letter told me the government
would mail cards announcing the ship's safe arrival in France.

Only one more letter came before he embarked, and I
almost wore this one out, wearing it next to my heart. For he
explained we should not discuss one subject until he did
come back because there was always a chance he wouldn't.
We could talk about that when we were together again for
the happiest moments of our lives.

The next communication was a card written on ship-
board and mailed in France. The government played down
the submarine danger as well as how poorly equipped our
army was and some other matters, but love has its own
knowledge and I had made that dangerous crossing hour by
hour until the card came.

The letters from France were less personal and fewer
in number. Most of them were undated and of course con-
tained no information as to what was happening to the unit

or where Jan was. My letters to him continued to be chiefly about our love and that magical future. Mine were uncensored as far as I knew whereas I finally realized his were thoroughly censored. Fortunately, a Lieutenant Frawley began to monitor them and soon not only became a close friend of Jan's but often added notes to me on the bottom of the last thin page saying he was looking after my boy! I cannot imagine a more sorrowful job than his and often wish I could have met him to say thank you for his cheering personal scrawls.

Dozens of the letters between us never arrived and only a few of the flood of packages ever made it. The news that Jan had been transferred to the Medical Detachment never reached me. It would have been a great comfort since I knew his temperament was not suited to any killing, even of small game, and I was never able to picture him machine gunning other young men.

One day Jan wrote that fifteen of my daily letters had just arrived in a bunch, after a month of none, and he gathered I still loved him!

One letter he wrote in January, 1918, partly escaped the censor's eye. It mentioned maple leaves in a Flanders field and his having been in the very town Joan of Arc was born in.

He described a wonderful old town on a hill surrounded by three thick walls, with a moat between each wall and with the towers of an old chateau overlooking it. He said it was his first taste of romantic France—but that all his thoughts were of the "House of Dreams."

As the war went on, Jan became more and more concerned about the future. When he came back, he now said, I would be a serious young graduate dreaming of being a writer while there wasn't much he could say for himself except that he was more sober and knew more about the world and was more than ever anxious to start working toward our future happiness.

There were five weeks when he was unable to write at all because the division was hiking all the time. I learned later that the men were crawling in the mud during that drive, and the casualty list mounting to the thousands. He never told me about this period or about the close friends who died. He only remarked once that you could only appreciate changing your clothes and having a bath if you had done neither for five weeks.

Eventually his corps was stationed in a village behind the front line, which I gathered when he spoke of being billeted in an old chateau owned by a Frenchwoman who felt sure his buddy, Hub, was trying to buy the chateau whenever he asked her how to get to the nearest village. These letters were filled with amusing anecdotes—about learning French, and playing poker with slips of paper for money when a bomb hit and scattered all the slips. He wanted to apologize for smoking cigarettes because they relaxed one. Would I forgive him?

One hurried note said his constant longing was to walk to his home and see a light shining from his wife's bedroom. This was another letter to wear over my heart, and it was probably a good idea the army YMCA paper was so flimsy, or I would have crackled as I walked.

He never mentioned Bill's death in the trench beside him—whether from fear of censorship or because he could not speak of it I do not know. He spoke of letters from our favorite high school teachers and of the excitement of receiving a copy of the Appleton *Post Crescent*, which he kept reading and reading. He began to sign such letters "Your football player" or "Your lover."

I wrote about the happy days we had had, trying to evoke that special grace of living. I stopped including daily events in the United States and wrote about what the House of Dreams would be like. I described a very nice but inexpensive little cottage, with climbing roses outside the bedroom windows and a red-checked tablecoth for the old pine kitchen table, and promised I would try to be as good a cook as Mama (quite impossible).

Some of my letters went in the trash can as being too emotional and perhaps upsetting. In fact, I practiced more discipline in writing them than I did in my creative writing courses (then called "Composition").

For us at home, there were no televised pictures from the front, no newsmen in trench coats reporting gains or disasters. The American population was kept in complete ignorance. I feel the truth is best, but the government had no such conviction. We never had any idea of what was going on in Europe or how many U-boats found their targets. We were to assume our glorious fighting men marched to victories daily, but my friends and I began to wonder why the war went on and on if this was the way it was!

I kept my letters from Jan in a sandalwood box. The packet was slim considering the length of time. I knew them all by heart but I still got them out over and over again, and the slanted, familiar handwriting arrowed into my heart. Most were written in a pale brown ink (where did the army get that?), and it faded rapidly, but so did the pink satin ribbon I tied them in.

The Armistice finally came. Jan had survived. But it was another several months before I saw him again for he was kept on in Europe for duties involved with the long and dreary aftermath of war.

It was late summer before the start of my senior year and I was home in Appleton when he arrived—at the same railroad station where he had left with the others those centuries ago. He was bronzed, strong, handsomer than ever. His mouth no longer curved into easy laughter, his sea-blue eyes seemed darker. I did not analyze this; I only lived in the miracle of seeing him again. As we threw our arms around each other, he was sweating with emotion, and the good warm smell of his lean body was sweeter than any perfume. It was sheer joy to feel my ribs almost cracking.

I am grateful we had a brief time together before I returned to college—a time of magic, almost drowning in happiness—for our impossible dream could not last.

At first I did not realize it, could not. I went back to Wellesley determined to face our separation bravely and confident that after one more college year we would be together for always. (It never occurred to me to drop out of Wellesley to be with Jan immediately. It wasn't done in those days, and besides, Father would never have permitted it for any reason whatsoever.)

Jan would be starting his first of four years of college. After that there would be more years getting established in a business or a profession. The lost time of the war could not be replaced. He had a long and difficult road to travel. It took many months for me to realize what that meant. Today it would have been no obstacle, but in those days it was.

We corresponded daily between Massachusetts and Wisconsin. But by the time I returned with my degree proudly tucked under my arm, the realities of our situation had become clear.

Young lovers today would find it hard to understand

why we did not simply walk away into the sunset together. But we were products of our time. Jan's uncle and aunt, fine hardworking Swedish folk, could not possibly subsidize his continuing education, nor the years it would take him to get established. Today it would be possible for me to get a job and support us, but in our town then, men were the providers unless they were physically disabled. A young man took on the responsibilities of a wife only when he could support her—and for Jan that was to be a long time in the future.

There was also the hangover from the Edwardian age when suitors got permission from the girl's parents before proposing. Very few young women—I do not remember any —married in our town without the blessing of their fathers.

My father had opposed my even going out with Jan from the beginning. I think now that Father was counting on an eventual waning of our love, in the face of so many obstacles. I do not know whether or not he actually came to a showdown with Jan. But in any case, I believe that Jan subconsciously may have felt that Father was right. As he saw it, he himself had a dubious road to travel and the idea of asking me to wait four or six years for him did not fit his ideals.

Jan made his decision without discussing anything with me. He simply withdrew during that summer after my graduation. I had to assume that somehow our separation had changed his feelings for me and he preferred to be free.

I spent a lot of hours waiting for the phone to ring. I did see him occasionally but there was never any talk about our future. I finally realized I had lived in an impossible dream, and it had ended.

I am now wise enough to understand Father's feelings

about Jan and me. But I had to be a parent myself to know the anxiety about the future security of one's child. During this miserable time only Mama kept Father and me from disaster. She was calm, gentle, wise, quieting Father's rages, comforting my fits of weeping.

The following fall I enrolled in postgraduate courses at Lawrence and began to teach part-time in the English department. Although I did not distinguish myself as to scholarship, I did eventually receive my master's degree.

Sometime during this period I heard from Jill, who was studying in Vienna—psychiatry, which was way beyond me— and had met a brilliant young American medical student. She married Max, and they came back to New York to live. He had more gifts than any one person should be allowed, as a surgeon, gynecologist and psychiatrist. Jill became a psychiatric social worker in New York, and their lives were complete when they had a beautiful baby daughter and a charming baby son. But that was a few years later.

While I worked toward my M.A. I wrote incessantly. I wrote first a great deal of poetry, which had rhyme and meter and was often in sonnet form because that form was difficult for me. I wrote short stories, also, because I loved the form. I kept a journal. I never saved any of this, but I was learning how to express myself, to communicate with someone outside of myself, even when there was no someone to know about it.

And so this era ended with the elms on the campus spreading their young green canopies over the mowed lawns, the ivy exuberant on the grey stone of Main Hall, and lilacs scenting the air unless the sulfur from the mills wafted in.

The day after Commencement, in the late afternoon, I walked downriver over the familiar path Jan and I used to take. The westering sun gave a translucence to the sky. The woods were as green as new hope and birds sang. I didn't then know much about birds, but I really tried to whistle back to them. A few rode the soft air carrying twigs and bits of string and stray feathers. I envied them having their own nests to build.

I began to think about my tomorrows, which I usually avoided like smallpox. One thing I had discovered was that I had a great love of teaching—something which had come down in the family since the days of Cotton and Richard Mather. I felt when I stood in a dusty classroom, facing rows of very young faces, much as actresses must feel when the velvet curtain goes up on the stage. Communicating with the students and widening their horizons was the most exciting experience imaginable. I looked forward to every class, loving the brilliant ones and cherishing the dull ones. If I could share a minute portion of what I knew, I was happy.

Today, from what I gather, not very many teachers have this burning enthusiasm, and I cannot help feeling the only really important factor in education is the gift of teaching, not the mechanical equipment. A roof, some desks, a blackboard, a little heat in January—these are all that are needed if there is a dedicated teacher. And when I hear about teachers' strikes closing schools for long periods, my first thought is that the lost days of teaching can never be replaced. I try not to think of the children with all that time dropping away like pearls from a broken string.

I was fortunate to teach at a time when strikes were no problem. There were none. Underpaid, overworked, with no extra benefits, teachers kept on teaching. It was a man's world then, so women never were paid equally. But the life on the campus was ordered, stable. Students did not riot;

they accepted the pattern. There were no demonstrations, at least not in our area, and the most serious problems we faced concerned whether to pass low-grade students so they could graduate or to uphold the academic rigidity as to grading.

However, I had no idea of what the next decade would bring to the halls of ivy. I only knew I had my happiest hours in the classroom. And I decided that day that I would like to teach always.

The one conflict I had was that I could not give up writing. I had no thought of ever being published; I wrote simply because I could not help it. I had a big wastebasket in my bedroom, and it was always full. As I finished one piece, I tossed it out, and when Father was not around, I carried the wastebasket to the trash container in the cellar. Then I began another.

Later, when I taught creative writing, I was often asked how one gets to be a writer. In the beginning all I could say was just to keep writing. Eventually I advised reading everything possible and trying to figure out how the authors managed their material, communicated their ideas and experiences.

Actually all life is a sharing. We have a choice only as to what we share. If we try to isolate ourselves from our fellowmen, we share our hostility. If we climb the desolate heights of a Kaiser or Hitler or Stalin, we infect nations with our paranoia. For no man lives in a vacuum; we are human beings bound to the same universe.

My perception, however, at that time was limited to a concern about what was to become of me, personally, and what I would do with my life. I would have to have some existence outside of teaching and writing.

Time would swallow me up, I thought, and nobody

would even know the difference. Even my students, to whom I gave everything I could, would never remember my name. They might say, "Oh, I had a good English teacher once. I don't recall her name."

As I reached this melancholy conclusion that afternoon, I came out on the bank of the river. There was the old man's shack, falling to pieces. One canoe with the bottom out lay on the shingle. Wild vines climbed over everything, establishing their own right to survival. The river flowed as wide and deep as ever, and the sound of the dam came like a vanishing thunderstorm. I sat down on a fallen log and watched the way the ripples lapped the muddy edge. There was nobody in the world except me.

I remembered my whole childhood then as the dark water turned to gold from the low sun. I remembered the endless traveling, the fears, the strange places, the brief security of high-school days, the terror of the war. I remembered my struggles with Father, and Mama's effort to establish some kind of stability between us.

Most of all, I remembered that day Jan and I went out canoeing, and the way he looked when he said he kept dreaming of being in a war. That was a dream that turned into reality so fast it was hard to recall how soon after that he was in the trenches.

I knew I was staying downriver too long, and Father would come home and call, "Where's Gladys?" I would have to invent some lame explanations as to where I had been. Mama would have supper ready and, in her quiet way, would be anxious. What was I doing sitting on that damp log, shivering in the rising twilight wind? I got up and brushed my skirt and started the climb up the overgrown path.

My town was spread out at the top of the hill, my town

that I was a part of, which had shaped me, given me the greatest happiness of my life and the most acute misery. I could not imagine what would have happened to me in another environment. It is not possible, I think, to live outside of one's surroundings. The truly great figures who have risen from the ghettos in my time have all been shaped by their background. Most of them never forget it.

Possibly in another part of the country, even then, Jan and I would have had a future. But we were locked in our own time, in our own place. There was no coral island lapped by a turquoise sea. There was no great metropolis, either, where life was freer. There was just our small town, with the great river flowing through it.

I did not consciously think about this then. I stopped to get my breath at the top of the path as I walked into the sunset. I did hear, for a moment, familiar words: "I love you, love you, love you." But they blew away in the river wind.

The exact moment when we change is seldom like lightning striking. Life is a business of growing, but usually we are not aware of it. We look back later and realize why we took one path instead of another.

That day I moved from one whole period of my life to another. I went home, walking slowly. I was cold and I buttoned my sweater. It was as if the circulation had stopped in my body. But as I turned down the curve toward home, I saw the supper lights in the kitchen and heard my Irish barking a welcome. He was psychic as most dogs and cats are. Father was already in his study stacking up the day's papers. Mama was at the stove, her delicate skin flushed from the heat and her soft cloud of dark hair stirred by the wind from the river window.

It was all as familiar as my own heartbeat. And I knew,

with a sudden awareness, that my roots were here. If I had
run away with Jan, I could never have set foot in this house
again, nor seen my mother and father, nor felt the warm
paws of my Irish pulling the threads from my sweater.

"Where have you been?" asked Father.

"Oh, I took a walk. It's a beautiful day."

Mama looked up and smiled, but there was a sadness
in her beautiful dark eyes.

"I'm glad you're home," she said.

We sat down to supper, and Father said grace. "It isn't
Sunday," he remarked afterward.

"I just thought fried chicken would be nice," said Mama.

"It's my favorite of anything," I said. "If I had to live
on a desert island and have only one thing to eat, it would
have to be fried chicken."

And so a section of my life was folded away.

Several months later, when Father was beginning to
worry lest I join the rank of spinsters, I met a nice young
Lawrence professor. According to the rules of society then,
a girl my age should be married. Frank's courtship presented
no difficulties. His field was music, and our music-loving
family spent many happy evenings while he played our aged
piano as it had never been played before. He was always
willing to turn from the great music to accompany Father.
There were no discords. Mama would keep the chocolate pot
filled, and Timmie sat on the sofa with me, thumping his tail
happily.

The wedding was in June, of course, and at home. Mama
baked the wedding cake. Father lugged armloads of green
boughs to decorate the living room. "Got to brighten things
up," he said, puffing.

I fixed a satin bow for Timmie's collar. One of Frank's friends from the conservatory offered to supply music, even though the old upright was hardly a concert instrument. Mendelssohn, of course, and Frank and I both loved Bach, so we added "Jesu, Joy of Man's Desiring." My wedding dress was made out of a piece of old ivory satin, and I used my grandmother's antique lace as a veil.

When it was over, we fortified ourselves with Mama's buffet—spicy baked ham, lime mold, feathery biscuits, strawberry punch. Then we took off for the cottage Father had built for me in Ephraim, on Green Bay. Timmie offered to come along, but Mama said that he'd better stay with her.

Times of serenity are as welcome as a clean sparkling day after a stormy night.

Over the Hills
and Far Away

WHEN I LEFT my beloved hometown, I did not realize how permanent the uprooting was to be. The house on the riverbank was home and represented the security I never had during Father's traveling days. I have, perhaps, an abnormal feeling for houses. They are personalities to me. I was always shocked when friends moved from one to another on a different street.

But about a year after we were married, Frank was offered a position as head of the music department in a very fine Virginia college. His career was the most important thing in our lives. The dean of the Lawrence conservatory would be there a long, long time and was excellent in the field. In order to advance in the academic world, one moved. This fact operates in education as much as in business, where often two years is as long as a young executive remains in one locality.

In all my childhood traveling we had never lived in the real South. I left most of our packing to Mama, who was certainly an old hand at it! I hated to see the open trunks and suitcases. The one comfort was that Father promised to ship Timmie to me as soon as we were settled. Mama said we would come back every summer and they could visit us and I would love Virginia.

Frank was so nervous about the move that he needed reassurance. He felt sure he could not manage being head of the department. His training was the best and he was a gifted teacher, but he was frightened. He, too, came from a small town in the Midwest and had gone to the University of Michigan, not far from home. He was sure nobody would like us since we came from the North.

Consequently we began our adventure more like exiles.

We took the train to Chicago, changed trains and rolled across the vast country, worrying every mile that we had made a fatal mistake in uprooting ourselves.

We rented a house near the campus and were immediately enfolded by the warmth, generosity and hospitality of the southerners, which too often is thought of as fictional. True, we were aliens, as I discovered when a neighbor asked me if we ate raw meat in Wisconsin.

"I never ate any," I admitted.

"Oh, I thought in the North you ate a lot of raw meat."

The head of the mathematics department found a cook for us because you had to have a cook. At that time, all work was apportioned. Husbands did not paint the house, or mow the lawn, or clean the cellar. I am sure this has changed with new life-styles.

Our cook, Belle, came from Nameless, a few miles from town, and was the first colored person (we called them that) I had ever even met. I loved her at once. She was one of the wisest, most compassionate human beings I ever knew. She may have gone as far as the fourth grade before she went out to work, but I felt in awe of her mind as well as her heart.

We had problems in the beginning. I could not see why she did not sit down at the table for supper with us. I also was greatly upset when we took the bus to the shopping center and she sat in the back instead of sitting up front with me. When I said I would sit with her, she turned an ashen grey as she shooed me to the seats for the whites.

I found the relationship between whites and blacks impossible to understand. They were completely dependent on each other, but protocol was observed vigorously. When the husband of Miss Larew's cook tried to kill his wife, Miss Larew sheltered her, confronted the man, protected the wife, made a judicious report to the police. But she and her cook never ate together.

My first crisis came when we had our dinner party for various members of the faculty. The men wore dress suits and were all handsome; the ladies looked elegant. I had a fine menu and also a new dress. Time went on, the guests sipped their drinks, and Belle did not turn up.

I finally dashed in and out of the kitchen and got dinner on the table before the phone rang. It was Belle's oldest daughter calling from Nameless to say her mother had fallen over suddenly.

"Has the doctor come?"

"Nome. We got no doctor here."

"I'll get someone," I said shakily, "and I'll be right out."
Then I called Dr. Terrill, our own physician. "My cook
is very sick," I said.

"Where is she?"

"She is in the cabin at Nameless."

"I'll be there as soon as I can make it," he said.

This would be the end, I knew. Nobody would ever
speak to us again. My poor husband, who was working so
hard, would be ruined. He was in trouble enough right then
at the dinner table.

I told the truth when I went into the candlelit dining
room.

"Well, of course you must go right out," said Miss
Larew. "We'll take care of things here."

And in a strange way that incident marked our acceptance in the community. Instead of being ostracized, we
now belonged.

Dr. Terrill probably saved Belle's life, although he was
not going to tell me, a woman, what caused the hemorrhage
or whether it was a stroke or not.

For a brief time, when Belle had to be away, I had a substitute. In fact, I had two different cooks. In my hometown
women did their own cooking except for the wives of college
presidents, heads of banks, or executives of the paper mills
across the river. I had no problems with Belle, for she decided on the menus and soon gave up even standing in the
doorway smoothing her starched, snowy apron as she con-
sulted me. However, the first substitute wanted complete
directions. I had begun to teach English Composition at the
college and was already out of the habit of doing all the

housework. I laid in an emergency supply of canned vegetables for the days I could not get downtown on the bus and
shop.

The grocer delivered most things, but choosing one's own
fresh vegetables was a personal job. As I dashed off to the
campus, I would tell Sarah Lee to open a can of tomatoes to
go with the chops and baked potatoes. She would serve lima
beans. I finally discovered Sarah Lee could not read and had
to choose the vegetables according to the pictures on the
label. I never went into the fact that tomatoes do not look,
even on labels, quite like lima beans!

The next substitute was Lizzie, who was one of the
modern generation. She was going to the local college for
black people. She seemed to study a lot rather than do the
chores, but I was pleased that she was getting an education.
She was even taking Latin, my favorite subject! Then one day
I came home early, and Lizzie was on the phone getting her
Latin from some fellow student who read the translation to
her. I was sick with disillusionment. Fortunately someone
dropped in for tea at that moment, and by the time I could
consult Frank, Lizzie had gone home.

"Look, you can't expect to transfer your ethics to Lizzie,"
he said sensibly. "She lives in a different social climate. At
least she has ambition."

When Belle came back, I hugged and kissed her. She
had a quiet gentlewomanly way of making me realize this
was not protocol, but she had to put up with it.

"Oh, Miz Taber," she said.

We made compromises in many ways. If we were alone
for lunch, I took my tray out and sat in the kitchen where I
could absorb her wonderful wisdom and gentle humor and
her compassionate way of looking at life. When life was too

difficult for me, I poured out my troubles to her and she restored me. She grew accustomed to the idea that I loved her as a person, and there were no walls between us. This was before the civil rights struggles, and the theory of white and black being equal was yet to come, even in Virginia, which was not like the deep South.

But it was a strange society, for the rules were rigid. There were "Whites Only" signs in many places, including restrooms at the railroad station, many eating places, all golf clubs and so on. The hospital had separate quarters for black patients. White doctors were reserved for the whites (unless, like Dr. Terrill, they took care of one's help under the most difficult conditions).

On the credit side, most of the white people took care of their help, even supporting them when trouble arose. If the yard man went off fishing and the lawn turned into a accepted. If the cook failed to appear, there was no confron-minor jungle, he came back when he felt like it and that was tation when she said she had the mizry.

As a Yankee, my only asset was that I tried to live in the society I was in with as much understanding as was possible. And I found my friends, both white and black, had a good deal of tolerance for an alien.

One of their main adjustments was to accept the fact that Timmie was shipped down by Father in a crate big enough for a tiger and actually slept in the house on the best sofa. He took up most of it, and guests sat around in chairs. He also developed a skin fungus and spent some time wrapped in bandages soaked in sulfur ointment which smelled up the whole house. House dogs, especially large ones, lived outside in those times, with runs and doghouses. Belle spent a good deal of time trying to remove sulfur ointment from the furniture. A few of my dearest friends were terrified of dogs. Their adjustment was amazing. Some of them even grew to love my Irish.

When they came for tea, I used my family silver, and Belle served watercress sandwiches. Timmie, wrapped in bandages, presided on the sofa!

My store of memories grew daily. In the North, nobody would call up with the grocery order, for instance, and say, "And please send your cat out. I have mice in the pantry."

To this day, also, I never cook bacon without remembering the Greek professor tossing a handful of bacon in a skillet on a picnic without even separating the slices.

"Turns out all right," said Miss Whiteside, and it did.

The natural beauty of Virginia was intoxicating to me. The Blue Ridge Mountains invaded the sky outside of town, magnolias bloomed, birds sang; in fact, the romantic stories about the South are not imagination. There is a special softness to the air, like realized nostalgia. And the pace of life at that time was not conducive to nervous tension. What you did not do one day could always be put off to another. There was always time to sit in the sun and visit.

I stopped making lists of everything I had to do at once. I also stopped turning up ten minutes early for any appointment. Clock-watching was not a prominent concern there. I hope it still is not.

Frank was never happier. His main interest in life was his music, and he had time enough to compose or give extra lessons to some gifted organ student without being tied down to the usual academic routines. He was fortunate to have some fine students who responded with enthusiasm to his gentle way of teaching. He did not have to immerse himself in the southern mores; he left that to me.

The housing shortage for faculty was extreme. A few of the older, established department heads were allotted pleasant apartments in the dormitories, but young single members had a hard time. This turned out to be a major blessing for me because we had an empty front bedroom which we rented to the Spanish teacher. After Ethel moved in, we formed a precious, lasting friendship. She was from Iowa so we had a bond right from the start. Our accents were so similar! But she had traveled a great deal and was more sophisticated than I would ever be.

She was slim and pretty and she walked with the staccato tread that small, slight women seem often to have. Her wit was lightning fast but never unkind.

She was supposed to eat her meals at college, but before long Belle began putting on an extra plate for dinner. She managed her classes with casual skill, and by the first summer vacation she took a group of her students to Spain. Subsequently, she took a group to France. She invariably lost the visas or passports and part of the luggage and mislaid reservations, but they all had a hilarious time. Eventually the American Express sent a manager to see her. He found it necessary to come again to straighten things out, and this became a routine. We felt the American Express was a fine organization to keep sending Charles from all those places his travels took him. Charles was a small, quiet man, impeccable in dress and manner, and we all had pleasant dinners together more and more often.

Ethel kept telling me she was never going to get married for she loved being independent and all she wanted to do was travel. So she married Charles and still did a lot of traveling with him. Giving up the teaching career did not bother her because, although she enjoyed it, she lacked that curious dedication to teaching that some people have.

Perhaps the greatest lesson she taught me was to take life with less intensity, and I shall always be grateful to her for that. Possibly my lesson to her was an appreciation of the fact that an Irish setter is an important furnishing for a home. Or that being domestic, as I was, need not ruin one's life.

I have a feeling friendships are never accidental but are destined. We go along with our customary living, perhaps always seeking subconsciously for friends who bring a glow to lonely hours. But the friends whom I have loved the most have never come because someone said, "I want you to meet so-and-so. You have so much in common!" Just a sudden casual meeting may bring a magical communion. Have we really met and known each other before? Is instant perception of another's personality possible, or have we perhaps walked together in some distant age in the golden isles of Greece or on a Scottish moor?

We first met our friend Murray Edwards at some reception which, as usual, had too many people and too little fresh air, two conditions which always make me sleepy. He walked in and someone introduced us. His colonel's uniform and erect military bearing made everyone else look a bit shabby and slouchy. He was not a big, brawny man and did not remotely resemble the pictures of army officers we see in photographs. He was slim and no taller than I, and my first impression was of quietness. He had come over from Virginia Military Institute, which was perhaps forty miles away, and I have no idea how or why.

Shortly after, he invited us to visit VMI, and we had our first experience watching cadets drill. They looked as fresh as a dewy morning and somehow vulnerable, as they proudly wheeled and marched toward tomorrow. Afterward we sat in Murray's living room, sipping punch and eating elegant snacks served by a starched servant. The room was so full of books there was not space enough for army decorations.

When he began to ride over for one of Belle's chicken dinners, we no longer had the curious feeling of separation between civilians and the army, and I gave up trying to dress for the occasion. Even when Timmie flung himself on that immaculate uniform, I did not worry.

Yet, the colonel was a very private person. He never reminisced about his childhood or his family. He never told us how he happened to choose an army career or what had led him to VMI. Most of the friends I have made are anxious to talk about their fathers and mothers and siblings, but he talked about world affairs or told amusing anecdotes about the school.

So he emerged in my life as a figure without the background filled in. Was it my overactive imagination that gave me the idea he had a tragedy in the past? I felt he had lost a wife, and once he mentioned a brother. But I do not think he ever even said where he was born and raised.

Yet our friendship was strong and close for all the years we were in Virginia, and saying good-bye to him was one of the hardest moments in our lives. It was especially difficult for me because I used to spend long hours with him, pouring out my feelings and experiences, and knowing he was always listening thoughtfully. He would sit straight and still in his chair, with a half smile on his face, his eyes looking directly at me. He always gave the impression he was at that time in my world and that what I said was important. If I ever bored him with my chatter, he never showed it.

I found with the Virginians as a whole a kind of openness which we lacked in the Midwest. The rest of the South I never experienced, but Virginia, for me, was an invitation to happiness, with the beauty of the surroundings and the easy way of living. The softness of the air was matched by the softness of the voices. Of all regional accents, Virginia's seems to me the most musical. It sounds like sweet water flowing through a piney woods. It sets me to wondering just how various parts of the country have such different speech—just how, indeed, every country has its own language. From time to time some specialist has promoted a universal language, which might advance the cause of peace. Meanwhile, diversity does add charm, at least to my ear.

When we went back to Wisconsin for the summer I was out of favor for a time because I had picked up a bit of the melodious Virginia speech. But I was not putting it on to emphasize my time in foreign parts. I had absorbed it.

It was in Wisconsin during the summer vacation that the baby was born. She arrived on time, but everyone said it was because I went to a Fourth of July strawberry festival the day before, and strawberry shortcake is my favorite dish. The strawberry festival was as traditional to the Midwest as the clam bake to New England. This one was perfect, for it was a good year and the rich, ripe berries were as big as plums. They dripped rosy juice down over the cake and golden heavy cream followed. Flaky biscuit dough supported both, none of this sponge cake.

Families gathered in the cool green shade where picnic tables and benches were set. It was a concession on the part of my own family to let me go, for in that time prospective mothers did not run around in public when they were obviously *enceinte* (we loved that French word) or "expecting." The expression "pregnant" had not become respectable. I had never heard it. The family doctor said, "My dear, I have good news for you. You are about to be blessed with a baby!"

Now young women flaunt their bright smocks or shifts with pride. They run around with hair flying, feet slapping the ground in sandals, arms and shoulders bare. I was reminded of the change recently when I took my kitten to the veterinarian. The waiting room was jammed, as usual, with Doberman pinschers, huskies, Gordon setters, assorted mixed breeds and a bevy of cats. One very pretty young girl sat near me hauling away at her large shaggy dog. During the hour and a half we waited, nobody paid any attention to her except me, although I wondered how we would all manage if she had her baby right there in the waiting room. I expected any minute to hear her cry out. Fortunately, she made it to the office and back out. In my hometown, not so long ago, she would have been lying on a sofa with a crocheted afghan spread over her tummy.

For the strawberry festival, I was garbed in what looked like a tent with sleeves. I wore a version of ground-gripper shoes (to balance the weight of the baby). It was one of those hot July days sweet corn loves, but I was covered up so only my head was visible. Father and Frank kept their distance, but mother stayed by me, embarrassed though she must have been.

I was too starving to care. I ate everything from fried chicken to fresh corn and several plates of that heavenly strawberry shortcake.

The next morning around sunrise I was rushed to the hospital. I had perhaps been in a hospital a few times to carry flowers to an ailing patient, but my ignorance of this huge, gloomy place was colossal. Only doctors and nurses came near me. The relatives were left in the lounge to pace around the potted palms or ferns. I knew I was dying, and nobody told me anything different. However, despite my sheer terror, I heard the desperate cry of my healthy baby girl, all nine pounds plus of her, as she rebelled at entering a cold, cruel world. I had one glimpse of her before she was whisked away.

I expected to go home the next day, and when I faced a whole week in the hospital, I broke down and wept seriously. That week was an eternity. The only music I heard was the chattering of sparrows in the ivy outside the window. The baby was brought in briefly, then whisked off before she could catch anything. Visitors tiptoed in and out. The family could look at the new miracle through a glass window. They agreed Constance Anne was the most beautiful baby ever to arrive on the planet.

I noticed she was lobster red when she squalled, which she did a good deal because she was hungry and not getting enough nourishment. Finally, eternity ended, which it seldom does, and the baby was wrapped in a bunting that was supposed to protect her from drafts but was hot enough to smother her.

Now I discovered every woman in town knew all about how to raise a baby. I was warned that if she swallowed air from the nursing bottle, she would die. If the hole in the nipple was too large, she would choke to death. If it was too small, she would strangle. If she had too much sunlight, she might go blind, but if she did not have enough, she would be weak as a slum child (we had no slums in Appleton).

I had troubles enough of my own. I spent all night jumping in and out of bed, covering her up and then uncovering her. Either a blanket was smothering her or she was catching pneumonia. I raised and lowered windows so often that only Father got a good night's sleep, and he could have slept through an earthquake!

I was afraid the milk was too hot or too cold, and I wasted a lot of it testing it on my wrist. Both of us smelled of milk day and night. Then there was the pacifier, which some said would push out her jaw and some said was necessary. I myself did not believe in pacifiers, but what did I know? The answer was absolutely nothing.

I did know there were germs waiting to pounce. I envisioned them as minute spiders. So I boiled the nipples until they fell to pieces, boiled the bottles, boiled the baby's gowns and my own and did the bedding up incessantly.

I was so nervous I leaped like a rabbit at the slightest sound, and poor Frank was obviously sick of the whole business.

Father was in a state. He could not mow the lawn at daybreak; it might wake the baby. And he detested confusion except when he made it. Mama did not wait on him hand and foot any longer, for she was trying to help me as well as do the housework and cooking (with no assistance from me). She was the only calm one besides Timmie, and even he was sometimes restless because nobody played ball with him.

Those artists who depict rosy, smiling babies held by serene young mothers in lavender frocks trimmed with lace certainly had never, I said furiously, had a baby themselves! And those smiling babies obviously never had colic. As for the beautiful young ladies, nonsense. I couldn't even get my hair waved, and I was too busy soaking milk out of my old middy blouses to dress up.

The only peace we had in the house was when it was the baby's bedtime and, accompanied by Frank, Father sang suitable lullabies such as "La Golondrina" or "I'll Take You Home Again, Kathleen."

Somehow we all lived through the summer, and in the fall we said those dreadful good-byes as the Chicago train came smoking down the platform. Father nobly suggested that Frank give up his job and we stay with him and Mama where the baby would be safer and would have someone to look after her. Mother said it would all work out. I said nothing because I knew how far away Virginia was and doubted whether we would live to get there.

Being perfectly healthy, Constance Anne survived the trip. She ate and slept and cried and used up a whole hamper of seersucker diapers. And Belle had the house ready for us. It was mirror-waxed, and a chicken dinner and a quart jar of delectable corn "likker" were there to restore us. Freed from his crate, Timmie tore the house down, so all was well.

The passage of time is like a view through a telescope, clear in the distance but never clear close up. Having babies today has nothing in common with my own experience, with the exception of the fact a baby arrives. When Connie grew up and married and had her first baby, I learned how wide the generation gap is. I looked back through that telescope to when my baby was born.

My daughter's pregnancy was utterly different from mine. I had read about natural childbirth, of course. But reading is not the same as experiencing. First of all, she did exercises helped by her husband. She did not lie down and rest with any old afghans over her. She dieted instead of being urged to eat extra nourishing foods for the baby's sake. She was checked by the doctor more frequently in one month than I had been in all nine months. And there was a spate of books to read about birth, babyhood, marital unity, psychological attitudes and so on. My own psychology courses at Wellesley never intruded on the subject of birth.

Furthermore, she went about her life as usual except for letting seams out in the charming costumes advertised so widely in *The New Yorker* and *Ladies' Home Journal*.

When the baby was imminent, I learned her husband would be with her the entire time. There was no necessity for the prospective grandmother to be on the scene at birth. And the hospital stay would be so brief there was no reason for me to make the trip in from the country to be there. I would have a phone call from the hospital.

The days of the whole family sitting in the hospital all night were over. I was confirmed in this when a dear friend called me up and said her only daughter, two states away, had a baby, and she herself had been invited to visit for a week *after* the young mother came home, mainly so she could do the cooking.

This modern way is better, I am sure, but it would not have worked in my day. Frank fainted at the sight of blood and would have been an extra hospital case. He barely survived with Mama's support down among the sheltering imitation palms in the waiting room. Father would have wanted to wreck the hospital if he had not been assured his darling would suffer no pain because of being unconscious from anesthetics.

As it was, the whole experience of Connie's arrival drove Father up the wall, as the saying goes. It took him longer to recover than any of the rest of us.

In Virginia, despite the lack of baby-care manuals and inoculations for a dozen diseases, Connie grew apace. Some of the early Virginia lore helped out, like sugar water for teething and rubbing the small gums with someone's family remedy. And Belle, out of the wisdom of her heritage, encouraged me to feed my child when she was hungry and not worry about the clock. "When she's hungry," said Belle, "feed her."

Belle also persuaded me that Connie was not going to die of pneumonia if a balmy southern breeze was blowing, and that I did not need to change her diapers (no disposable ones then) every half hour. Belle boiled them up daily and hung them in the brilliant sun to "freshen up."

Belle allowed as how the baby would not care if there was extra noise in the house, so Frank could practice the piano all he wanted and we stopped tiptoeing. We also began to have friends in for tea or even dinner, and finally dared to go out when Belle stayed over to baby-sit.

We even had a weekend visitor when our old friend Barre Hill came down from Chicago where he was studying opera with Mary Garden. Tall and dashing in his ankle-length raccoon coat, Barre brought boxes of gourmet delicacies and a suitcase full of arias. When he gave us a concert after dinner, Belle had an honored seat.

In other words, we gradually got back to a rational existence, and I stopped leaping up every hour all night long to check on the baby.

The feverish devotion to vitamins had not arrived, but Connie grew with all the vigor of wild violets in May. Her babyhood whisked by and before we knew it she was teaching herself to read. This did not astonish us since I had done the same thing as a small child. Some earnest psychologist friend wanted to test her IQ at the time and found only one question that bothered her.

"What is a plumber?"

"Oh, that must be the man who fixes the piano."

Just how we had gone so long without having to call a plumber did surprise us no end.

Going to kindergarten ended the babyhood era but was chiefly notable because she met a boy. The children in the neighborhood who were her own age were all girls. She told me his name the first day and added joyfully, "He wears a lavender up-top!" Whether it was his sex or the lavender up-top that gave him his charm, we never knew.

The school was, of course, all white. So I finally persuaded Belle to bring her daughter Violet over one day. Belle simply ran out of excuses. Violet was a very pretty child, scrubbed and polished. Her dark pigtails framed her brown face. Connie's delicate, blond, feathery curls and fair skin made, I thought, a charming contrast, and I got out the old box camera and took pictures of them, none of which came out.

But that day led to trouble, for the other children in the neighborhood would no longer play with Connie. Their mothers would not let them cross the street.

"They can't play with me," Connie sobbed.

I could not imagine what had happened and finally went to see Miss Larew, the mathematics professor, whose wisdom was not confined to math.

Over a glass of mint tea, Miss Larew figured it out. She also solved the affair with dispatch. She went calling in the neighborhood and casually mentioned that Belle was Connie's mammy and Violet just came along with her mother. The next day all the children whooped over and the yard once more erupted with giggles and squeals.

Then I understood a good deal more about this mysterious society. Friendships between black and white children were expected when the black mothers operated the way Edwardian nannies did. But there had to be a sanction. Black and white did not casually mingle.

I also learned that the way to avoid conflict in a community is to consult those who are indigenous to the area. If I, an alien, had confronted the neighboring women, I would have been met with blank stares.

"We don't know anything about it. Our children associate with whom they feel like."

And I would have decided there was something dreadfully wrong with my offspring. Was the boy with the lavender up-top to be her only real childhood friend? If this had gone on, I might have been a ripe candidate for a charm school for my daughter.

As I think about the time in Virginia, I know it widened my horizons beyond expressing. Many great writers have come from the South, and I have read as many as I could. My personal Virginia was unlike theirs since my roots were in New England and most of my growing years in the Midwest. I was a traveler in this country, and my profound love for it came from daily experience and not because my ancestors owned great plantations and were related to the Lees and Stuarts and someone who was a sixth cousin was from the Washington side of the family. There was an elegance to the southern inheritance which did not pertain to the rugged men who founded the New England colonies.

There was also, as I felt, a pride in people with a background of poor whites, sharecroppers. Among the black friends I made, those stemming from slavery were a special aristocracy, as was quite right since the slave trade flourished by stealing the best, the young chiefs.

The past had not gone, in fact. Whenever I met someone, I was told the history of the family, which nobody in the North ever thought of mentioning. I found it fascinating, although at times troubling.

"Some of the Colonial houses in New England are just as they used to be," I ventured.

"You never had Sherman's march to the sea. Our plantation was on that march line," I was told at once.

As for the land itself, I found that even the most romantic of the southern writers described it more reasonably than I could. There were the Blue Ridge Mountains cresting against a great sea of pure sky. They were never the same from moment to moment as the light embraced them with love. Below the mountains, the rich green valleys gentled into the distance.

The towns and villages were always at full tide, with color from gardens, shrubs and overarching trees casting green patterns on sidewalks. I never learned the names of the myriad flowering bushes, but when the magnolias were in bloom I was dizzy, and the roses, roses, roses seemed incredible. I felt a botanist or naturalist might perish from the excitement. The rich soil—even the red soil—and the gentle climate made everything grow and blossom extravagantly.

Then there were really mockingbirds. They were not fictional. My friends accepted them as just a few more of the hundreds of birds in the surroundings but to me they represented the romance of the old South. I had never seen or heard a mockingbird before. A good many of the southern birds were strange and seemed to sing a lot. Now I have mockingbirds in my New England yard, and whenever I fill the birdbath for them (they wash incessantly), I think about Virginia.

Even in midwinter the softness of the air seemed to be

there. Perhaps I only imagined that it was so fragrant, but the season of flowering was long and the autumns gentle.

Fortunately for my idealistic viewpoint, I was never in Virginia during the intense heat of summer since we went north to our cottage in Ephraim, Wisconsin. It was often already hot as school closed, and I wilt in heat faster than a faded rose. Mint-julep time came early in those days. And people carried fans to Commencement!

Our main problems were minor. The white mouse Connie brought from school had to live in a large bird cage in the pantry off the kitchen. He (or she) rapidly developed into an enormous rat with no ideas of friendship. Belle did not adjust to the idea of a rat in her pantry although she was patient for some time. I myself, who love almost anything that breathes, never got to be cozy with him. My poor husband never went into the pantry at all.

Every animal has a scent; most are very agreeable. Timmie, when not shrouded in sulfur bandages, smelled like a new-cut clover field. My cats have a soft, mysterious sweetness conducive to burying one's nose in the satiny fur and sniffing. My current wild skunk friend has a slight odor of musk, far different from the suffocating smell of a panicked one. But this huge white rat did not have an attractive aroma. In the end he was transported back to school.

The two canaries were an experience. We had them in the dining room in a sunny window. I did not really want them for I feel allergic to caging anybody or anything. (As Connie once said later, we all live in cages in a way.) Our two canaries started fighting as soon as we got them. The dining room was usually full of pale golden feathers, so when company came for dinner our last-minute preparation was sweeping and dusting the dining room. We tried separate feeders. They tossed seed around and went on fighting. We bought a second cage and separated them. The dining room was not very big, and the cages and stands took up half of one side. Then they sat and glowered at each other. We were, in short, stupid, and it took a biology professor to point out that our two small, angry birds just happened both to be males, a fact the seller had never mentioned. I have often suspected he had his own troubles in the shop with them.

We found homes for them separately and settled into a quieter life with our Irish and a small aquarium of goldfish, angelfish and casuals. The aquarium was my husband's pet project, and he discovered fish are not so simple. I was determined not to get attached to them, but when one or two fish floated dead on the water, I worried. Was the water too hot or too cold? Was the food all right? How often must the tank be cleaned out and aerated? This was before the day of the gadgets that you stick in the tank to purify the water.

The neighborhood was full of stray cats, which we fed on the back porch so they were no trouble, except there were more and more of them as time went on. Even those with homes dropped in at suppertime for something special. It was no wonder, for the prevalent theory then was that a cat will not be a good mouser if you feed it too much. My belief is a cat is a mouser if it is a mouser—as Gertrude Stein said, a rose is a rose is a rose. And an entire diet of mouse is not one I recommend.

We were living as if there were no tomorrow. It was a secure world and a settled one. The only shadows were cast by the sea-blue mountains at sunset or by thunderheads cresting over the valleys. Faculty squabbles had no intensity, for the new era of educational conflict was not yet upon us. No student protests shook the leafy campus; no radical professors were ever fired as far as I know.

The college spent full time on teaching, and I am old-fashioned enough to be grateful that that particular student body only missed classes on account of illness or a death in the family. There is, I believe, a rhythm in learning which it is better not to break.

That whole period in my life seems like a tapestry, a blending of infinite colors and composed of an infinite number of threads woven to make a whole. Then suddenly I was back in my early childhood, for we were packing to move. Frank had developed a hearing difficulty, which turned out to be a progressive condition due to a faulty operation when he was very young. Teaching music became increasingly difficult, and even faculty meetings were hard for him to follow.

The steamer trunks were dusted off, cartons lugged from the grocery, rugs rolled in burlap, china packed. I gave away much of the furniture and small treasures I had accumulated. I was in a state of shock, quite aside from personal anxiety, for my roots were deep in that red soil. Frank accepted the whole business with more stamina and less worry, for he was certain that when we went back north his hearing would be restored miraculously after consultation with specialists. He also had not formed such a passionate relationship with the place or with our friends as I had. If he had, we could have shared our experience and I would have been less lonely.

Furthermore, I have come to know we never really escape or outgrow our backgrounds. I now regressed into mine, into the fear of being uprooted before I fitted into whatever place we lived in briefly. I had really believed the quiet campus in Virginia was a permanent anchorage. But my husband had grown up in one white house in one small Michigan town with a bevy of sisters and relatives around and his father's clay products plant as solid as any Gibraltar. He went to school there, then to the nearby university. His hitch in the navy had been interspersed with leaves back to the hometown. The move to Wisconsin had not been like a basic uprooting but a branching out, and going home from there (for Michigan was always home) was easy even in the days of slow travel.

Consequently, the move to Virginia was his first major one, and he was slow to put down roots. But once he got used to the soft southern accent instead of the flat midwestern one, he found himself in a familiar world. He taught the same courses as before, the organ and piano were the same, and he was comfortable. Giving up his music would be tragic. Giving up his home in Virginia would not.

I woke in the night after nightmares in which I sat in a musty train wondering where we were going, with visions of dingy second-floor apartments, adobe houses, boarding-houses. And a haunting fear of the future, a dark, dripping cave ahead. If I had been optimistic about an easy restoration of my husband's hearing and some stable environment for my child, I would have been better off. The conflict between feeling I was once more a small, frightened girl and realizing I was an adult with responsibilities to two people kept me in a state of eroding fear. This was long before F. D. R. said we have nothing to fear but fear itself:

Friends did all they could, but they really made it worse because the thought of leaving them was an added nightmare. The lovely farewell parties often left me limp as wilted lettuce. I knew the ties being broken would never be re-tied, although there was much talk about our coming back to visit and keeping in touch. Distance and the passage of time frays the strongest of bonds; although friendship may be for a lifetime, friends need contact with one another.

I stored up, in the last days, every moment from sunset over Blue Ridge Mountains to the song of the mockingbirds, the laughter at a faculty party, the potpourri smell of the air. I collected memories as avidly as an archaeologist collects artifacts of a bygone age.

Belle wanted to come with us. She promised she would come when we were settled. Saying good-bye to her was one of the most difficult hours of my life. I cried against her starched bosom. She comforted me as well as she could. Fortunately, we were alone because crying made me hiccup so that I sounded like a series of firecrackers going off.

The door finally closed behind us. I am sure carpenters who install doors do not stop to consider what they mean. An open door may lead to unknown delights or sorrows; a closed door symbolizes an end.

I could not dig up any favorite quotes from Keats or Shakespeare, but what kept flooding my memory was entirely sentimental.

> Guarded by encircling mountains
> Beautiful and blue,
> Stands our noble Alma Mater,
> Glorious to view.
> Lift the chorus, speed it onward,
> Ne'er let praises fail!
> Hail to thee, our Alma Mater,
> Randolph-Macon, hail!

Since I cannot carry a tune, it was as well I sang quietly to myself, or my husband and daughter might have left me behind. Both of them were looking ahead to a summer at

Ephraim, in Door County, in the cottage my father built
for us next to his own. There was no rush, Frank decided,
about visiting those hearing specialists.

We were driving in order to get the car back north, and
the car was so full not even a Kleenex could have been added.
The tires were not very good, but the garageman said they
might get us through. There were no superhighways then so
we bounced along, stopping to add water to the radiator
from time to time.

The best memory I have of that trip was when we
stopped in a small midwestern town and a waitress with a
heart of gold advised me *not* to order the lamb stew for my
daughter.

"It is no good," she whispered.

There was one thing to be said about travel in those
days. On today's superhighways the only way to know your
progress is to check the mileage. At that time you saw the
country, all of it: drowsy little towns, green meadows with
pure unpolluted streams flowing by, cornfields greening in
the gold light of the sun, cows browsing endlessly (cows do
eat a lot).

You rode to hilltops and saw this country spread out,
rich with farms. You went through twilight valleys with rivers
shining on their way to the sea. I had a feeling I seldom
now experience of the vastness and splendor of my land. It
was a world with no exit signs or toll booths. The man at
the village grocery store drew a map for you with the stub
of a pencil.

And once we agonized through Chicago, we knew where
we were. We were heading for Milwaukee and Appleton
and, finally, north to the summer cottage on Green Bay.

"When are we going to get to Grandma's?" asked
Connie, plaintively.

Summer's Lease

THAT PARTICULAR SUMMER was as variegated as an antique patchwork quilt. We were rootless, yet deeply rooted in the past. We were back in Wisconsin in the cottage in Ephraim. The little white village stood so quietly overlooking Green Bay. The people, mostly Swedish and Norwegian, moved without hurry. When the Chicago boat docked at the great wooden pier, there was no great hullabaloo. The sound of the church bell in the Moravian church spire only made the stillness deeper.

Perhaps Ephraim already belonged to yesterday, for even the few telephones—operated by a hand crank and with a live operator at the other end—were scarce and not much used. Our dear friend Dr. Reeve did have one in his summer cottage, but the rest of us went to the village to make any calls.

Summer visitors could stay at the Anderson House, which was really an old, big white house, not an inn. Nobody had heard of motels. The meals served at Anderson's were so memorable that some folk came there just to eat all day. There was no cocktail hour, and it was not missed. The warm, homemade crusty bread, the newly picked vegetables, the fricasseed chicken with fluffy dumplings, the fresh-caught fish, the cherry pies—these and many more delights were unforgettable.

Captain Anderson had been a seafaring man and still walked with the gait of one used to the roll of waves. He looked like a gentle version of a Viking and was probably the most beloved man in the village. I believe he owned the main pier; at least he managed all its business.

Door County was famous, then, for the sweetness of her cherries, which either because of the soil or the moisture in the air were bigger, sweeter and redder than any others I ever ate. They had a faintly spicy flavor to temper the sweetness, and the dark juice spilled in your mouth when you bit into them.

During cherry season everyone burst into activity, even the summer people. Mama had a hand-operated cherry pitter, and even Father helped pit the cherries for canning and preserving. Cherry pies, cherry tarts, spiced cherries and something called cherry bounce were just a few of the results.

Since the bay was not polluted by speedboats and tankers, the fish were plentiful. You could drop a line from any shore and have a fine catch. Grilled or baked or in rich chowder they kept homemakers well supplied.

We also had wild mushrooms since Father knew all about them. They were plump, tender, a warm ivory in color.

In this one aspect of Father's reckless personality, he was supercareful. I suppose the scientist came out in him. We never had one dubious mushroom.

Whatever nonlocal supplies came in, they came by boat or in an open truck from the town of Green Bay, since there was no railroad. Mail was picked up at the village post office when anyone remembered to go for it.

Our cottages had fireplaces for heat, kerosene stoves for cooking, Aladdin lamps for light, water from a bubbling spring at the foot of the slope. A covered wire box in the brook below the spring was the icebox.

The outhouses were trim and modestly set back in the pines. For baths we took bars of Ivory soap down to the lake, or if it was too cold we used a tin foot tub, heating the water on the stove.

There were no huge highways on the peninsula then and not many country roads. These meandered through villages, cherry orchards and the deep green of the woodlands. They often ended at the shining waters of Green Bay, where it was possible to picnic without climbing over beer cans and dead sandwiches.

For other recreation, there were church suppers where the food never gave out, even after a fourth helping! When I tried French cooking in Paris much later, I never found it equal to those church suppers in Ephraim.

If one ever got hungry in midday, the ice-cream parlor offered homemade ice cream, churned by hand and made with real cream. The ice-cream parlor chairs must have gone to collectors by now. Then, they were just metal chairs with a design of curves and spirals forming the metal backs. The tables were round with firm metal legs and white metal tops. They, too, have moved into elegant decorator apartments and homes.

Colored postcards were sold at the parlor, so while consuming double scoops of ice cream, one could write "Wish you were here" to outsiders.

Green Bay was the nearest real town and everything could be purchased there, from clothes to Kaap's creamy chocolates, but most of the summer folk stayed put in Ephraim. It is now known as the home of the Green Bay Packers, who really began as a local affair. I still follow them faithfully even though Lombardi has gone.

Life was a kind of waking dream, bright and serene, except of course that wherever Father was, there was excitement. Our land abutted on the State Park, a huge untouched area including Eagle Bluff, woods, and shoreline. The only sandy beach was there, for most of the shores were rocky. The one concession to so-called civilization was a rather shaggy golf course (where much of our best mushrooms came from).

The park was run by a state superintendent named Mr. Doolittle. He and Father were born to be enemies, and their feud has never been forgotten. Father's attempt to move the sand beach to our shore by rowboat and Mr. Doolittle's conviction that our cottages were on state land, no matter what the deeds said, did not make for amity. Both Father and Mr. Doolittle believed they owned the land, and Father, who among other things was a surveyor, once resorted to stringing barbed wire along the boundary, which Mr. Doolittle opined was illegal.

However, the summer we came back from Virginia, Father had more on his mind than Mr. Doolittle. Conflict blossomed like a forest fire in our snug cottages. I have always noticed that when disaster strikes, people bear it better if they can blame somebody. If one is ill, he or she did something to *bring it on*. If one dies, the doctors or the hospital are at fault. I am sure if we had been in an earthquake,

Father would have said we should have had more sense than to be at that spot.

But he had trouble blaming his son-in-law for the deafness which was disrupting all our lives. For this son-in-law did not drink or smoke; he ate moderately and never indulged in the kind of foolishness Father did, such as trying to chop down and lug a giant tree single-handedly or carry tons of boulders to build a dock. Frank never lost his temper when he was shouted at (partly because he did not hear it). He had done nothing to deserve his affliction. I was a poor target, too, at this time, and so was his innocent grandchild.

This left God, and that was a major problem. Father's rather stormy personal relationship with God had never been so threatened, and he was not able to either make his peace with the Almighty or be sure God was responsible. His only release was to badger Mama, who bore it with her usual calm wisdom.

"Rufus is upset," she said.

I now feel the greatest sympathy for my father. In his tradition, a man supported his family, laid aside ample money and retired only when death opened the door. But Frank was still unable to face the uncertainties ahead. So here were three members of the family suddenly without income or security, and with no visible concern about the future. The prospect of supporting us all the rest of his life gave Father nightmares.

Unfortunately, his son-in-law had no consciousness of money. He assumed that somehow it would be there when needed. This attitude is characteristic of many artists, as I now know, but it horrified Father.

Between the two of them I was torn apart. I had my own terrors about the future but I did not plan to make life any more difficult for Mama than it was.

There were many plans suggested. Father felt he and
Mama should take over Connie. I was not going to be bereft
of my one child. Father decided we should all move in with
them. My husband said no. Mama said nothing.

In the end Frank came up with his own plan. We would
go to New York City in the fall, where those mythical big
specialists might perhaps restore his hearing. He was already
corresponding with the League for the Hard of Hearing. We
would spend one year in New York, after which we would
go back to Virginia, buy a house near campus, and all would
be as before.

There is, I believe, a rhythm to everything in nature and
in mankind. So it was that summer, when suddenly tempers
cooled as if the thermostat had been turned down. Circumstances had not changed, but we had. Father began to sing
again, his pure, high tenor coming from the beach where
he moved boulders around. Mama lost the tight lines around
her beautiful mouth. Connie played her imaginary games,
dancing in and out from cottage to cottage on butterfly feet.
Frank and I swam, sunned on the rocky shore, unpacked all
the books we had brought, walked in the woods on the pine
needles that were so soft and smelled so sweet.

We picnicked at Little Sister Bay where the beach was
made of stones, rounded and polished during the glacial age.
We filled baskets with them, pink and pale blue and silvery.
It was said this was the only beach of its kind. We decorated
mantels and tables with the small stones. We made doorstops
with the larger ones and lined the steep path to our own
beach with them.

We also picnicked at Eagle Bluff, where there was then
a ledge that gave us the feeling of being in an aerie with
the great green water below rippling to the horizon. We
took friends there for sunset parties and ate golden sweet

corn roasted in the husks. Even I, who am so afraid of heights, felt serene there and never worried about being swept over the cliff and dashed to pieces on the rocks below.

Sometimes I went out in the rowboat with Father to fish. I usually managed to catch enough for supper, but Father, as usual, never left his line in long enough. He never wanted to stay in one spot because he was too restless, and he rowed so fast I always expected the oars to bend!

The rest of the family stayed peacefully on shore, but Mama kept a wary eye on us in case Father tipped the old boat over. We were an odd sight, I know. I wore my bathing suit, which was a complete costume down to the knees. Father wore old pants, a white shirt with the tails flying, and a straw hat. His fair skin burned and blistered in the sun and he sweated heavily. Below the hat brim his mop of reddish curly hair was always wet.

In spite of the fact that I was always cross because he was so impatient to move, and that his feelings were hurt because I caught most of the fish, we had a wonderful time. I retrogressed to my childhood, when I used to toil after him in rows of corn while we hunted arrowheads, or struggled behind as he loped through the woods, or waded in Lake Winnebago while he splashed in and out of the water hunting specimens.

He never went anywhere without finding some treasure, and he could always tell me how it came to be there. Even scratches on a boulder marked the progress of some glacier and the composition of the rock where it came from originally.

This summer Timmie alerted us with a special bark to the presence of black snakes. And he could not resist investigating porcupines, but one bout with a skunk was enough. He was in the water so much that he looked like a mahogany seal most of the time. If he found a dead fish on his way home, he bore it in triumph to lay at our feet. If Father decided not to take him out in the boat and left him in the cottage, he unlatched the screen door and swam out. The sight of Father trying to lift sixty-five pounds of soaking dog into a tipping boat a quarter mile offshore did give Mama a headache, but I was sure both Timmie and Father could swim across the bay, if necessary.

In that period, cocktail parties were nonexistent. Afternoon tea was the social hour and it was especially for the ladies. Even in Ephraim, Mama used soft linen napkins and teacloth, real silver and china. Since she had to wash the linens by hand and iron them with a sadiron heated on the Perfection stove, this was not an easy chore. She polished the silver regularly. And no teabag ever entered her domain. She steeped the fine English tea in a teapot, rinsed first with boiling water. A fine silver strainer took care of the tea leaves.

She was an imaginative cook and her delicate bite-size sandwiches were famous (my favorites were the watercress). The tiny cakes were iced pink, white, chocolate. She made candied orange peel for extras. The ladies wore flowered light summer dresses and carried lace-edged handkerchiefs or imported embroidered ones in white summer purses. I think of the faint scent of lavender when I remember them.

The faces of the guests had a kind of innocence, dusted only lightly with rice powder. Rouge and lipstick were common in Virginia but had not yet appeared in Door County, although some advanced gentlewomen rubbed rose leaves on their lips.

Some long, dreamy summer afternoons a few close friends sat on the porch (not a patio) and snapped their embroidery hoops over their handiwork or knitted, ivory needles clicking happily.

Conversation was less than profound. Women did not

discuss sex or liberation or politics. If they were frustrated, I did not know it.

There was, of course, plenty of tragedy. But nobody "died," they just passed away or went to their reward (I wondered what reward for some). The general feeling about difficult husbands was expressed as, "Of course that is just like a man!"

Meanwhile, the men puttered with their boats, or fished, or cut firewood or went swimming, turning up to take their wives home in time to get a good, rib-sticking supper.

Children had no regimented sports schedule; they played on the beach or swam as far out as allowed. Teenagers walked in the woods or bicycled to the ice-cream parlor or gathered on Anderson's pier to watch the Chicago boats come in. I do not think there were any courses in anything, not even tennis. Youngsters taught themselves to swim, row boats, even paddle a canoe if the parents could afford one. They did not realize how underprivileged they were, for the great age of specialization was just a few years ahead.

The family was a unit, dominated by the father and usually run by the mother, but the battle of the sexes which so embroils our current age had not begun. And about the only drugs in circulation were aspirin and Epsom salts.

Probably this was the last summer of innocence, at least as far as I know, and our own family enjoyed it, perhaps with more intensity because the future presented such a problem. We clung to the familiar pattern. We even read by the light of the Aladdin lamps at night or sat watching the moonlight on the water. Sometimes Frank played for us on the elderly upright piano.

When the first crisp tone of autumn came, we were appalled. Where had summer gone? It was falling away with the first drifting leaf. The bay took on a deeper color. The

sailboats were gradually facing a winter on land. I felt sorry
for them, for once upended onshore they lost their grace and
freedom. I had a strong sense of identity with them, for I
too was losing mine.

Now birdsongs diminished but the scurrying of squirrels
and chipmunks made a pleasant sound as they busied themselves storing up for the bitter winter ahead. A good deal of
their industry was responsible for the growth of new trees,
which people who shot them never stopped to consider; they
were the enemy for they did break into cottages during the
winter and usually wrecked them trying to get back out.

The land was, as always, green with the darkness of the
pines but there were stands of white birch in Wisconsin then
and the pale gold birch leaves fell like sunlight. The sea-blue
chicory gave way to deep red of sumac along the roads.

The air smelled of smoke as householders burned the
rakings from their yards. A few intelligent folk saved the
leaves for mulch and compost, but this was, on the whole,
not a saving age for gardeners as the land itself was so rich.
They just "cleaned things up," as they said.

Since human beings respond to the rhythm of nature
as well as nature itself does, families squirreled about tucking things away. The age of mothballs has gone, I think,
but at that time mothballs reigned supreme. First blankets,
rugs, linen were sunned on a benign day and then layered
with mothballs and put away. Some householders even tossed
mothballs all over the cottages as they left, presumably to
asphyxiate squirrels or bugs. Then oil was poured from the
lamps—in case of fire—although how a lamp with oil in it
could suddenly explode, I never figured out.

It was my job to wash all lamp chimneys for both cottages and wrap each one in brown paper sacks. Mama
scoured and scrubbed everything and Father cut and stacked

wood to season over winter. He still wore his summer long underwear and on warm days sweated heavily. Connie was busy tucking away the summer treasures—shells, Little Sister stones, silvery bits of driftwood. My husband had the job of sorting cartons of manuscripts and packing suitcases and boxes and organizing books. He was, in many ways, the most organized of us all and he also enjoyed his chores. I hated mine. Mama did not really enjoy shutting up the cottages and Father was very short-tempered. Timmie was nervous, as he always sensed change and thought things were fine just the way they were. He brought in as many extra dead fish as he could find roaming the beach and always came in dripping just as we finished waxing a floor.

There are two theories about leaving a place. I believed in just going when you had to, because when you got back you could take care of everything then at leisure. It all had to be done over anyway. My parents held the opposite view.

"What's the use of doing all this?" I asked Mama one exhausting day.

"One never knows," she said. "We must take care of everything."

One single unlaundered tea towel left behind would have worried her all winter.

"I don't see why we have to sun all those blankets when the first thing you do when you get back is put them out on the line," I said.

"You wouldn't leave them *all* winter without it!"

The worst were the Perfection stoves, which were so hard to clean at best. By the time we were through with them, we hated to use them even to boil water for a cup of tea. I do not know what Mama used to prevent them from rusting over winter, but I hated the smell.

Toward the end there were the farewell parties, which

were a sorry attempt to combine gaiety with melancholy.
The summer people scattered as far as Chicago, except for
a few professors who went back to Lawrence. The resident
population stayed happily in Ephraim and how I envied
them! Without the migratory people, they led freer lives and
they did not mind being snowed in or having a temperature
of thirty below.

Connie's best friend was a blue-eyed, golden daughter
of Ephraim, and Connie suffered at the thought of leaving
her. Ultimately she inherited Connie's elegant dollhouse
which Father built, and I am happy to think it is still on
the peninsula and still in use by children there.

The time came when the keys were turned in the locks
and we walked up the hill, so deep in pine needles. The day
was blue and crystal, and the last sound I heard was a scurry
of squirrel in the pine tree beside the outhouse. The bay,
when I last looked, was still and the deepest green-blue ever.
The little brown cottages already looked abandoned, as
houses always do when their hearts stop beating.

"Hurry up," Father yelled. "If we don't get started,
we'll never get there!"

But I walked slowly. I knew something was going out of
my life, never to be repeated. There was a finality about this
leaving, an echo of the departure from Virginia. The rest of
the family also was upset at going and Father, as always,
took out his emotions in being cross while Mama said nothing
but kept busy tucking Timmie in with a beach towel in case
he felt chilly on the long drive.

I am sure one person was completely happy to hear the
chugging of motors for he would be rid of Father for a whole
six months. Mr. Doolittle would have no competitor.

As I remember it, we had only one flat tire on the way

back to Appleton and Father was used to patching flat tires and blowing them up with a hand pump. He never wanted any help so the rest of us stretched our legs and gathered rusty goldenrod to take home. We stopped in Green Bay as always to stock up on delicacies at Kaap's.

Looking back on my life during that bouncing ride, I had time to think. I formed a conclusion I have kept that there always are more ends than beginnings, although this does not seem right. I was grateful for the summer, which gave us all a respite and a time to reach into ourselves. Whatever was ahead must be faced with as much spirit and grace as possible.

Once again, as in my early childhood, I was to be uprooted, but I now appreciated Mama's incredible courage in the life she led, and I prayed for a small bit of her stability and gentle strength. I had taken her for granted all these years and now I knew her. I would at least try to be worthy of being her daughter.

It was sunset when we drove into Appleton, and the little town was dipped in gold. The maples and elms gave forth their own light from the brilliant reds and russets and yellows.

Father only noted that the confounded lawn needed mowing again, even now. We unloaded the tons of baggage and Mama got on her ruffled apron and unpacked groceries so that savory smells soon came from the kitchen (we never *ate out*).

I went to the edge of the hill and saw the Fox River flowing quietly into twilight.

Summer's lease, I said to myself, hath all too short a date.

The Other Side
of Yesterday

OUR APARTMENT was in an ancient building in upper Manhattan. It overlooked Amsterdam Avenue and West 106th Street. There were four rooms, a shadowy kitchen, a living room the size of a good cigar box, two bedrooms and a bathroom with a tub on claw feet.

During the seven or so years we lived there, various managers came and went, but whether they owned the building or were employed by the owner I never knew. The Rosenbergs were the couple who carved themselves deepest in my memory, perhaps because during their incumbency the whole building began to show the signs of decay and neglect.

The pipes leaked. The stove sent an aroma of gas through the whole place. The heat went off when days were cold but burgeoned in midsummer. Windows buckled in the wind, soot lay deep on the sills. We were on the top floor, which turned into an oven in June and a refrigerator in January.

There was an elevator, which crawled asthmatically to the sixth floor when it was in the mood. My claustrophobia was encouraged when it stopped flat midway. Any complaints made to Mrs. Rosenberg met the same response. She flung her arms in the air and cried, "I do the best, I do the best." Her best usually meant doing nothing.

Mr. Rosenberg was the invisible man. If he ever surfaced at all, he was scuttling away, leaving the field of battle to his wife. I could not speak Russian; he had problems with English. I never knew how the Rosenbergs happened to be living on Amsterdam Avenue because in those days I was too timid at the mere thought of dealing with landlords, and now I am sorry for I imagine their story was a fascinating one. We were all exiles from our own world so we had that in common.

Mrs. Rosenberg was a small, rather plump, very dark woman with a mop of black hair and wary eyes. She lived drama and whenever anything went wrong, which was dreadfully often, she was ready to attack, arms flying, voice throbbing with emotion. I was no match for her, that is certain.

I hated to step in the kitchen, not only because the smell of gas made me seasick, but the sight of cockroaches scurrying to get under the refrigerator and behind the stove terrified me. To me, they seemed worse than the Wellesley mouse—but perhaps it was really that I had never gotten over that.

Also, I had a severe sense of guilt for having brought my
only child into this stony jungle when she might have been
safely at home in the gracious house by the Fox River.
Father was right as he often was. But the maternal instinct is
not reasonable. I felt being separated from Connie would
give me one of those fading deaths Victorian ladies were
prone to. I would be in "frail health" and then die.

My readjustment to the new life was not hastened by
the fact that everything I did was wrong. My attempts at
budget meals only reminded Frank and Connie of the wonderful meals Belle used to cook. The vacuum cleaner hated
me. Laundry piled up in the bedroom closets. Wax turned
into jelly on the furniture. When it hardened, anyone rash
enough to put a hand down got stuck.

Connie's days at school were miserable. She was a for-
eigner. Her accent labeled her and her clothes did not fit the
mode of the city. There was nobody to play with.

It took me quite a while to realize what was basically
wrong with my efforts to create a peaceable kingdom in this
city. I had an incurable defect: I could hear. I could hear
that proverbial pin drop. Naturally my husband resented this;
how could he help it? None of the magic treatments were
helping. Once I understood this, I was much better emo-
tionally.

There was one special blessing we had which we did not
really appreciate fully until much later. Jill and Max and
their children were in the city and were not far away as distance went, although worlds away in terms of circumstances.
They lived in an enormous apartment on Central Park West
which was, I suppose, part of one of those fabulous mansions
of the early days. They had room enough for both children,
themselves, Max's mother and a live-in cook-housekeeper.

Max had an office across the park which was so elegant that I felt embarrassed to walk in. But it came to be a haven, for he was never too busy to spare some time. Max knew the best specialists in the field who might help my husband. He could pick up the phone and make things happen that might otherwise have taken weeks and weeks for us.

He also, in some offbeat way, persuaded me that I could not help being able to hear so well.

When it became evident that no miracle operation would cure Frank's deafness, we did what people always must do; we accepted it. Frank painfully wrote our joint letter of resignation to the college, and we tried to decide what to do next. Staying in New York, at least for a while, seemed to make sense. Frank would study lip reading and perhaps eventually get a teaching certificate. The League for the Hard of Hearing was of inestimable value, for they had lip-reading classes and also courses in all kinds of artistic fields not dependent on ears!

The best thing about the League, as I came to know, was that it made my husband part of a group—all kinds of people in all walks of life, but all with a hearing difficulty to bind them together.

His artistic ability turned to decorating and his beautifully designed gold-leaf tinware opened a whole new career to him. The visual world of beauty now belonged to him.

Meanwhile, I kept on writing, which was not exactly to my credit but was my own solace. I had always planned on a Ph.D., and I worked at the university with the dream of doing a thesis on the Brontës which would really be "definitive," as critics say.

I was fortunate enough to meet Helen Hull, who taught creative writing, and I took courses with her as much as possible. She was a major influence in my life, for she suggested I send in some of my short stories to the magazines. When my first check came in, it was for $250 and we celebrated with a juicy sirloin steak.

The thrill of seeing something one has written actually in print in a leading magazine is beyond my power to describe. Later, when my name was on the cover of five separate magazines the same month, I was not nearly so excited!

Miss Hull became a close friend as well as an inspiration. I learned as much as I could, even over lunches and dinners. When she suggested I write a novel, of course I did. I would have written it anyway but would never have ventured to send it to a publisher. When it was accepted, we had another celebration. And at that point I gave up on the Ph.D. since I learned it would cost, at that time, a thousand dollars to publish the thesis. It would also have meant two years more of study. Frank agreed with me that if I could get paid for everything I wrote, it was better than paying ourselves.

Our major worry, aside from adjusting to his handicap and to our financial insecurity, was that Connie did not fit into the mammoth school in the city. The sophisticated, smartly dressed children viewed her much as a pack of wolves would a small rabbit. She never complained for she was a valiant person and possessed great intuition about the family situation, but she withdrew more and more into herself. Even when she won a scholarship and was able to attend a fine private school, she did not belong to the group. But she kept on learning all she could and acquired an academic background which served her well at her university.

This is a time I wish to forget for I longed to have her experience the kind of high-school living I had known in Appleton. Perhaps today she would have been a dropout because she was not happy, but at that time she simply worked harder and learned more! I liked to think she inherited from her ancestors an ability to survive as they survived the disastrous journeys from England to the New World.

One cold day when I was having trouble with the ending of a short story, the buzzer sounded and I went to the door. There stood Belle. I thought I was hallucinating until her warm arms folded around me.

"I thought maybe you needed me," she said, "so I came."

Never having been out of Virginia, she had managed the trip. Violet had married, her relatives were for once in good shape, so she just came! Few events in my whole life have moved me more.

The cold fact that we could not support her or put her up seemed so minor. I only knew she was there, this warm and wise woman who had been our rock and refuge during the years in Virginia.

It was too unbelievable for me to ever write about, but it was real. When I stopped clinging to her, I had coffee with her. She bustled around the dingy, gas-smelling kitchen, cleaning up and muttering to herself softly about the mess there.

I telephoned Jill.

"No problem," she said calmly, "we can use a live-in housekeeper and she can come with us."

So Belle and her luggage were carried to the big apartment on Central Park West, where she had a good room with a view of the park. She ran the household with her usual skill and grace and eventually did much of the home nursing for Max when he developed leukemia. He was determined not to be in the hospital where he had worked so long, so a hospital room was set up in the apartment. Nurses were in and out but Belle was always there. Toward the end, he looked at Belle and said, "Belle, am I going to die?"

"I think, Doctor, that is just between you and God," said Belle.

And he smiled at her.

When I read now about race problems, I can only feel sorry for racists who have never had a Belle in their lives! How much they have missed and how sad it is!

About this time, Timmie died and Father buried him under a shady tree by the river. The man who protested about getting a large, unsanitary pet planted daffodils on the grave. To me, it marked the end of another era in my own life. It was a long time before I could speak his name. I thought of that dark mahogany fur I had put my head on so often for fourteen years and of his flying grace, incredible intelligence and devotion.

I cannot remember how long it was before Jill suggested I should have a cocker spaniel. An Irish setter, she said sensibly, would not be happy in the city, with no fields to skim over. Central Park was not enough, nor walks on a leash around the block. Cockers adjust well to city life and are small enough to fit conveniently in a small elevator.

We bought Dark Star from the Norman Thomases on Long Island. The Thomases lived in a pleasant, rambling house on a quiet road. The yard was full of cockers and Mrs. Thomas made her way through them to welcome us. She was a charming, slim woman with flyaway hair. She wore a tweed skirt, a casual blouse, and both her long stockings had runs in them.

"Just imagine Mrs. Thomas being like that!" I said.

"Well, she was cleaning out the kennels," said Jill. "No matter how famous her husband is, she is not afraid to work."

We briefly met Mr. Thomas and I decided if all Socialists were like him, perhaps they should run the country.

Star was as black as Mama's jet beads, round as a ripe peach and wiggly as a catch of eels. She was seven weeks old and was not a show prospect, but as I carried her to the car I couldn't have cared less. We paid, as I remember, about fifty dollars for her, which seemed a lot of money.

On the way back to Manhattan we stopped for gas. The minute Jill opened the door, a small black bullet exploded from it. It took three garagemen, a couple of bystanders and us to capture her and save her from being smashed to bits on the highway.

This trip was an omen, for Star was always in trouble. We began housebreaking her to papers, but her idea of a bathroom was any soft rug or comfortable easy chair, or the middle of our bed if she happened to be on it. It was my first experience with a dog who refused to use nice shredded newspapers. Her IQ was astronomical but so was her stubbornness. When I wasn't carrying her to her papers (after every meal, between meals and whenever I was in the middle of working on a piece of prose), I was crawling under the bed or sofa and mopping up while she watched happily.

We could not soak the whole apartment with disinfectant to discourage her, but we did our best and it was not good enough. She sometimes went so far as to play games with her papers, tossing bits all over. She chewed them up. When I came in from a hard day conferring with magazine editors, she met me at the door, a wagging, ecstatic bundle of joy, and then followed me as I crawled around the closets scrubbing spots.

Attempts at discipline did no good, except to upset me! Rewards were welcome when she happened to be at least in the vicinity of her papers but otherwise made no difference.

Shutting her in the bathroom was a disaster for she screamed at the sight of a closed door between her and me, and since her voice was louder than an opera star's, the neighbors in nearby apartments complained. Meanwhile she made trails of the bathroom tissue and chewed scallops into the edges of the bathmat.

When she was old enough to go outdoors, she loved it and skipped blithely along the street, but always waited until she was at home to go to the bathroom. About all we could be thankful for was that she was a small cocker and not a Saint Bernard.

A few years later, Jill and I were visiting J. Latimer Rees, one of the great early cocker breeders and trainers. He was a chunky, rosy man with bright, twinkling eyes and an easy smile. I told him about the struggle I had been through and asked what I had done wrong.

"Nothing," he said, tilting his chair back. "Her mother was the same way. I knew her well. You could have taken her back."

"Not for all the gold in the Indies," I said.

"And you did win out in time," he commented.

I did not, I thought, win out. But Star eventually trained herself because she grew tired of that particular game.

She never did accept the vacuum cleaner, however. I could understand this since my feud with vacuum cleaners was endless. The cord always sprung at me and wound itself around my ankles, or it sneaked back of the table and coiled around the legs. The motor part whisked ahead and banged the desk so pages of manuscript flew off. Sometimes the whole appliance stopped dead and I discovered the plug had fallen out all by itself.

I worked hard at that time to keep the place so clean

the vacuum could sit quietly in the bedroom closet! An old-fashioned carpet sweeper and a dust mop and a broom helped a lot. And Star enjoyed all of them.

We bred Star and she had her first jet-black puppy in the middle of the night, which seems to be the correct time according to nature. While we dozed a few moments, she left her elegant whelping nest and went under the convertible couch. We had to help with the birth lying flat on our stomachs holding flashlights, so it was fortunate everything went well.

I was thankful the new baby took to house-training without a quiver. In fact, the rest of Star's puppies were no problem, which makes me believe she and her mother had some kidney difficulty which never showed up in examination but involved a delicate connection with their emotions. Even in our own stolid selves, most of us react at times of excitement by finding the nearest bathroom!

About this time, Jill decided their apartment was lonely without a resident cocker, so she and I made another expedition on a Saturday and came back with Blue Waters Ripplemark, a black and white male puppy, a breeder's dream as to temperament and conformation. Aside from eating up a chunk of linoleum from the kitchen floor, he was no problem.

"He's too good," said Jill. "I keep thinking the good die young!"

"He reminds me of a bank president," I said. "One you could trust, consult and revere—not a big-city banker but a small-town one."

"What's wrong with big city ones?"

"They don't have time for depositors worried about fifty-dollar checks."

Where Star had enough sheer charm to get an airplane off the ground, Rip had a kind of steady sensibility. She was eccentric, he was stable. When she barked at the repairman, he wagged his tail in welcome. Star was extremely jealous but Rip always waited patiently to be picked up. Fortunately, Star was fond of him, and the small black one often curled up against the big black and white when they napped together.

By this time not only our cockers but our two families were almost inseparable. We had adopted each other at both age levels, and it was a merger that remains to this day, though now I am the only one left of the first generation. On sunny Sunday afternoons, we went to Central Park with the children and the two cockers and began to imagine how it would be to have a place in the country for weekends, with free runs through sweet meadows, walks in leafy woods, picnics by a trout stream. It was the germ of a dream.

A dream can be nourishing, even an impossible one. And we needed it, for World War II was a reality as well as a nightmare.

There were never to be any more wars on this planet; we had been assured of that. So I just happened to have the small radio turned on as I wrapped Christmas presents on that December 7. I was alone and doing my best to tie uncooperative ribbons (no stickums then). A sea of colored tissue paper was spread on the bed.

Disaster strikes me numb, and I was still sitting there with the scissors in my hand when the family burst in. It had to be a giant mistake! Tomorrow everything would be all right. One war in a lifetime was one war too many; this was some kind of savage hoax. But when the phone rang, Jill's voice was quite definite.

"Have you had the radio on?"

"Yes, I was wrapping presents," I said, stupidly.

"Another war," she said. "Max is coming home from the hospital."

Then I sat with my head in my hands, opening my heart to all the grief and terror and tragedy beginning again.

The ultimate strangeness of wartime is that life goes on away from the battlefields. I had learned that at Wellesley. And I suspect that during the French Revolution those who lived then still went about daily living. Man is made of stern stuff. Getting food, heating frigid homes, protecting helpless children—these occupy people even when bombs rain down.

The young and beautiful went off to be killed. Parents cried in the night. Young lovers prayed. Packages were mailed abroad that seldom got there; censored letters were mailed and lost. Shortages were common. Liberty ships pulled away to Europe. War bonds were sold. Innocent Japanese-Americans were dragged into our version of concentration camps (a national disgrace, hard to forget).

And ultimately the Manhattan Project was under way with eminent physicists such as Einstein, Teller, Fermi, Oppenheimer and others whose names I cannot remember. The atom bomb would be developed.

Frank was teaching the deaf and working part time at a war plant. I mended and canned and wrote.

The main contribution Jill and I made directly to the war effort was to be Air Raid Wardens. New York City was an attractive target and fear was at flood tide. My memory of that time is hazy, but I recall climbing out of bed on black nights and walking the streets with my flashlight or

climbing the stairs to the roof to scan the sky while the moon
shone peacefully as ever. The darkened city was a new world,
the towers of Manhattan penciled against the sky. I was always tired and my feet hurt and it rained a lot or the wind
blew street litter in my face. It was also bitter cold or broiler
hot.

But the feeling of satisfaction at doing something needed
made the experience worth the discomfort. The fear that one
night the bomb would fall was always with us, but the can-
yoned streets were not yet invaded by the tide of crime so
we never expected to be mugged or shot or raped on Amsterdam Avenue. It was even safe to walk past the neighborhood bars.

My feeling for this giant metropolis changed and grew.
The darkened apartments had occasional gleams of light
where shades or shutters were cracked, and I liked to think
that behind those chinks were families, children sleeping in
the innocent security of childhood, parents sipping beer, pet
dogs and cats curled on shabby couches (it was not an affluent neighborhood).

I had discovered before this war that a city is not one
colossus but a conglomerate of neighborhoods, small communities. I knew about Harlem since Jill was one of the
head social workers there. I knew, of course, about Fifth
Avenue, the theater district, Greenwich Village, Chinatown,
the elegant area on the East Side where the extremely rich
lived when not on cruises or in Paris, Rome, London or
Saint-Moritz.

But my own neighborhood was none of these. There was
the laundryman and his wife who ran a small establishment
around the corner. They were Russian Jews, come as im-
migrants to the United States. They were soft-voiced, gentle

people, always cheerful although their dark eyes still reflected the suffering of the past. When we came to be friends, they once brought out all they had saved from their former homeland, a set of goblets, delicately chased, solid, pure silver. To hold one was like having a butterfly in my hand.

The greengrocer across the street was an Irishman, tall and straight and with the gaiety we used to associate with the Irish. Mr. MacNamara would never let me buy a few chops or a head of lettuce unless he was sure they were absolutely fresh. He was not a hardheaded businessman making profits whenever possible. I used to stop in often just to hear about his childhood. He missed the cottage he grew up in and especially not being able to wake up at dawn and hear the chickens scratching in the thatch on the roof.

The corner bar could not be described as a dive. The round, rosy German owner was never to make a fortune out of the family men who stopped in for a beer after a long day's work. I forget the name of his place, something like Ye Olde Tavern. He sold sauerkraut, hard rolls with salami, bottles of wine. Ladies did not sit down at the red-checked-tablecloth-covered tables until much later, but wives often went in and carried out brown paper bags of pickles, rolls and so on.

There was a small radio shop run by a man who could only speak Spanish; my own Spanish was long gone, but my daughter had no problem chatting with him later on in his own tongue.

The streets were littered; soot sifted through the air and lay deep on windowsills. Fire sirens sounded all night long and ambulances also split the night with sound. The apartment buildings were old and showed their age. Some had been elegant residences at the turn of the century but

were later chopped into apartments which housed everyone
from Columbia professors to subway workers. Pipes always
leaked, ceilings cracked, paint peeled from the corridor walls.
We had plenty of exercise climbing six flights of stairs when
the shaky elevator would not run. On the coldest winter
nights the furnace always went off. On hot days the windows
stuck. And I do not remember their ever being washed outside, as long as we were there.

A city has her own climate. It is colder in winter, for the
winds roar down the streets and the sun has a hard time
reaching down to thaw the dirty snow. On hot days the
stone, brick and steel absorb the heat all day, and night is
never long enough to cool them down. In neighborhoods like
ours there were no trees to make peace with nature and no
lawns to hold the rains and snows. The New York flower
seemed to be the geranium in our area, for valiant pots
stood in a good many windows trying to absorb the sooty sunlight. More affluent neighborhoods went so far as to stand
potted palms in the lobbies. I never could get a single house-
plant to grow and suspected the leaking gas from the stove.
("I do the best, I do the best.")

Central Park was a haven, and we spent as much time
there as we could. Sometimes we walked on the narrow,
greening area along the Hudson, although even then it had
an odd smell. But we loved the Cloisters Museum best, for
it had a walled garden with real flowers. The building looked
like the Middle Ages, and within its stone walls a small
museum displayed its treasures in the dim, cool light. There
I saw the famous medieval tapestries, and the ivory unicorn
in a woven world of green trees and rainbow-colored flowers.
I felt as Keats did when he first looked on Chapman's Homer
when I first saw this dazzling stretch of tapestries. The chil-

dren soon began to call the unicorn my unicorn and were patient about waiting while I stood trembling with delight.

A third haven was a tar-roofed, ancient building in lower New York where a dear friend, Nadine Stein, had a top-floor apartment. She had been a favorite friend of the doctor's and Jill's. She was a slender, dark woman, the kind who seems forever young. Her hair was short and black and straight as silk thread; her fine-boned face was the color of oak leaves in midwinter. Her eyes were so beautiful one felt like drowning in them. I cannot now remember just what kind of artist she was but I remember those eyes.

Her apartment had a shabby look, which was somehow charming, and a ladder stairway that led to the roof, presumably for escaping from fire. I am sure there was no outside fire escape on her floor. Nadine used the stairs to climb to the roof, where she had created a small roof garden in pots, pans and boxes.

She had a few rickety garden chairs and some small tables. We used to picnic there, and for Jill and me this roof was our escape from the cage of the city. There were no skyscrapers in that area, only warehouses and junk shops and a few one-story shops, so we could see the whole sky, and the city below was only a tumbled mass, remote and no longer oppressive. The few towers that reached toward the sun were beautiful. Only in summer the tar roof melted in the hot light and the smell drove us down. A faint smell of tar followed us, but it was cooler inside.

One of my cherished memories is the day Jill and I went there to have lunch because we wanted to hunt in the junk shops for treasures. It was a hot, molten Sunday and our families decided as one to stay in upper Manhattan where it should be cooler. They also thought the long subway ride

was silly, as it certainly was on such a day. Nadine assured
us everything would be open because Saturday was the Sab-
bath down there.

Somewhere I had seen a piece of milk glass and with my
usual lack of common sense decided I would collect milk
glass the rest of my life.

"We won't live in the city forever," I said, "and I can
take it to the country house."

"What country house?" asked Jill.

"Oh, an old house or a barn in the country where we can
all go weekends. The children can make snow angels on
clean snow in winter and walk barefoot on dewy grass in
summer and pick wildflowers."

So perhaps I should thank the milk glass and that particular ghastly trip on the subway for a dream!

After a lunch of salad, French bread, cheese and cool
pink lemonade, we set out on our hunt. I found walking endlessly on the hot pavement exhausting. I was sure my shoes
were cooking and my knees ached impossibly. I panted along
behind Jill—it seemed to me I never was even with her no
matter where we went. We poked around in dozens of places
full of everything today's connoisseurs would faint over.

And then, just as it happens in a fairy story, we went
into the last place, obviously an old warehouse taken over by
a secondhand dealer. Jill was looking covetously at an antique Franklin stove and discussing its past with the dealer,
who assured her it was a choice piece worth at least $10 (no
less than $250 now, I think). She wanted it but there was
no chimney in their apartment or any way to put a stovepipe in.

So I was the one who found something. I absently
lifted up an old, smelly piece of burlap. Dust and insects

rained on me, and the odor of rats was stifling. But as I backed away, reaching for my handkerchief (I always carry one), I saw a white gleam in the midst of the debris.

Even now as I look at it, I cannot really believe that white gleam was my swan compote, perfect, not even chipped! I picked it up, cradling it in rather shaky hands. The swans seemed to be swimming around the bowl and they breathed. Like many of the oldest pieces, this was uneven and tilted to one side on the round, semipedestal base. The color was that of the very old glass, opaque yet lustrous. It was like moonlight on snow in a piney woods. I stood in a trance holding the compote against a thudding heart. I knew this was really old for the feeling is different from the modern copies—it has something to do with the kind of sand used in the early days. Modern pieces copy the old but also have a kind of shine that old pieces do not have.

"It's time to go," called Jill. "Almost sunset."

I walked to the lighted front of the warehouse and held up my treasure without a word.

"How much is it?" asked Jill, practical as always.

"It's a fine piece. Twenty dollars. Worth a lot more but seeing she likes it—"

"We'll take it."

Between us we managed to scrape up the money and still have subway fare. Of course we could not afford twenty dollars. But I came to a conclusion then that I've held since, which is that if you want something badly enough you should get it, and then pinch and skimp afterward as long as necessary.

Wrapped in a dirty, yellowed newspaper, my treasure rode back on the subway. I must have felt the same emotion as a prospector feels when he pans for gold and finally finds that lump of precious metal. Or like an archaeology expert who digs up a piece of grubby bone that turns out to be another missing link. Or like the botanist who discovers a totally new species of wildflower at the edge of some hidden meadow.

I suspect, as I think about it, that what one collects is not as important as the feeling of collecting. It is good to hunt patiently for something special and experience the triumph as the collection grows. Always the first object will lead to another and another. One friend has a valuable collection of old bottles salvaged from dumps. Another collects the green glass things once used on telephone wires, and one man collects ancient automobiles and has so many the whole place is overflowing with them. I have my milk glass, beginning with the swan compote!

There was an extra blessing on that special Sunday, for I wrote a short story called "Eden on a Rooftop," which one of the big magazines published and for which I received the astronomical sum of $350. It was a very simple, romantic story about a young girl who was exactly like Nadine except for being twenty years younger. She lived in an apartment under a tar roof. She had picnics with the hero on the rooftop and they ate exactly what we always did.

The plot was the same as in most young love stories and all I really made up was our hero—and it is easy to make up a hero! It ended happily, complete with a moonlight night and a soft wind blowing the heroine's hair when he kissed her.

I unconsciously established my credo for writing at that time. It was, and is, to write only about what is familiar. Use your own experience to build on. The basic material must be your own.

This is difficult to explain for a story may begin with a simple snippet of conversation one overhears at the meat market or something a friend says which reveals an inner self. One of the most successful stories I ever wrote came from a small incident and seemed to write itself. "Legend of Lavinia" came from a casual discussion between two gentle ladies who lived peacefully together in a house belonging to one of them. They never argued or bickered as most folks do, until the second lady inherited a quarter board which had come down in her family. She wanted to put it on the wall in the parlor. Quarter boards that came from the prows of early ships have the ship's name on them, often embellished with gold designs. I never saw this one for the friend who owned the house said flatly, "That thing can never be hung up in *my* house!"

It was put in the barn.

"This is the only thing that was my own," said the second lady.

It seemed to me this symbolized a relationship that is very common in people's lives so I wrote about it, and the editor liked it almost as well as I did. We named our automobile Lavinia when we left the city and got one.

This kind of experience led to my second credo for writing, which is to observe everything in the world around you and feel something about it. This makes the craft a hard one, for you never stop working day or night. No matter how tiring it may be, you keep on looking, hearing, thinking, feeling with and about people and places. At night you lie awake recapturing the slightest detail of the day. Nature herself is an eternal challenge for it is not enough to say snow is falling without trying to study just how the flakes fall and how, for instance, a juniper tree looks with her feathery green pointed tip frosted over. It took half a day of staring at a blizzard to compose one sentence to express it—the white darkness of snow finally came to me, for that is exactly what it was.

Authors who say vaguely that it snowed or the sun shone are not for me, and I even stopped reading what was otherwise a pretty good book when the characters walked under falling leaves when it was obviously only August!

"The next thing, he'll be tapping sugar maples for sap to make maple syrup in May," I said to Connie.

This is a harsh judgment but since this man was evidently purely urban, I felt he should keep his characters in the city. Writing about the city is complicated enough, as I learned when I tried to do it in the years we were stuck there.

I tried to show the city without analyzing it and to feel with the whole of the giant metropolis. For the final objective of a writer is to feel so deeply that the feeling communicates itself to the reader. In real life we spend most of our time trying to communicate with others; in a story or book we must. The fundamental drive which makes one write is an aching need to communicate.

So I was possessed with the need to identify with the city and share everything about it. Nothing could be more impossible, of course, for the city is a cosmos and never a unity. Every individual in the millions has his or her own city.

For instance, if I lived ten lives I could not convey what part religion played. I think every religion known to mankind is practiced in New York as well as countless spin-offs. My own experience was confined to Riverside Church, which was theoretically Baptist but included a great congregation of Protestant believers. My family had founded Congregational churches in the early days in New England, but I was currently a Methodist for the reason that Father loved the dynamic young Methodist minister in Appleton. Jill had been raised in the Scotch Presbyterian tradition. The doctor paid no attention to sects but had his personal belief in an infinite power. My husband felt the same God belonged to every man.

We joined Riverside Church, which was really a cathedral. I found such an enormous church and such a mass of worshipers strange. I was used to a small church where everyone gathered outside after the service and discussed the sermon and made plans for the next church supper or the Ladies Aid Bazaar.

And inside, although I appreciated the magnificent music, I kept remembering the little church where Father's voice soared on high wings over everybody else's while the organist struggled with one creaky pedal no matter what she did. Mama made no sound since she sang off key as I always have, and so she only pretended to sing in church, but her silk dress whispered when she stood up, and the faint scent of lavender sweetened the air.

It was no fault of Riverside that I felt alien there. It was my fault, for I never tried to join any of the church groups or take part in church work. And with hundreds of people coming and going, visitors to the city, the regular members could hardly sort them out.

The one member of our two families who did take part was Jill's daughter, Barbara, who decided to be baptized in the church. She had not been baptized as a baby and now in her subteens she joined the sessions of instruction and in due time was ready for the ceremony. Her brother, David, refused to have anything to do with it and Connie had been carried in my arms to the altar in Appleton when she was no bigger than a rabbit.

There was a baptismal font underneath the floor behind the pulpit. It was really a pool, large enough for the assistant minister to go in at one end while the children went in the other and they met midway. When not in use, the floor was put back and I used to wonder how the minister felt preaching above water!

As the hour approached for the rite, the four of us were as nervous as any parents could possibly be. The awesome solemnity was too much! But when the assistant pastor advanced in his flowing robes and stepped down into the water, my sense of reality returned, for as his robes floated I could see he wore rubber boots.

Then the children came and there was Barbara in what her brother said was a white nightgown. Her soft, dark hair fell over her shoulders, her deeply blue eyes were solemn, her sensitive lips pressed tight. She looked like one of those delicate attendant angels in some medieval painting. As she stepped forward, I had a sudden terror lest she slip and fall flat in the water but she made it safely and the pastor pushed her under and she came up like a drowned mouse, water streaming from her fall of hair.

Jill's lips regained their normal color, instead of being blue. The strangeness was still with us, as if Barbara had been on a far journey. When dried out and dressed and back with us, the mystery lingered, as did the radiant look on her pale face.

"I couldn't go through this again," Jill whispered.

The sunlight outside seemed brighter than usual and the sound of the city louder. But the congregation looked natural, the women with elegant hats, rainbow frocks, white gloves, the men in sober grey or dark blue, the children dancing about, eager to be off. As we looked back at the church spires yearning toward the sky, I felt suddenly that perhaps we were not alien anymore but had a shared experience with every single person who had been inside that morning. All the parents, I was sure, felt as we did, wondering about what the future held for these youngsters, hoping, fearing, praying for a world that could forget war.

One facet of the giant city became very important to me as time moved along. It was, in fact, one more world inhabited by editors. My first approach to it was about like leaping into a volcano. As any woman would do, I bought a new dress, hat and shoes. I found my gloves (I never wore them) and carried them draped casually over my new bag. I had my hair done.

Frank said I looked rather like a bobcat. He had a point, for my naturally curly hair did not take easily to the beauty-parlor hairset, not even after the college struggle with marcel waving. Connie added just one word. "My," she said as I started out.

There is, after all, nothing to bolster one's confidence like the family! A brief chat with my agent did not help.

"Now, don't let him scare you," he said. "He does have a reputation of sending authors out in tears but I can tell you he is the greatest magazine editor in town."

I had troubles all the way. The subway was jammed and the smell made me sick. My flowered hat, perched on all that hair, kept sliding down over my right eye. I caught one heel on the subway stairs and just missed falling in the greasy muck. I was not at home in high heels so I scuffed down Fifth Avenue, walking like a crab. Beads of sweat from sheer nervousness dripped down my face to streak the makeup. And, finally, as I slid through the great doors of the sanctum, I lost one glove.

I spent the time in the elevator (I hate elevators, too) trying to make one glove look like two. By the time I was shooed into the editor's office, I was about as miserable as a woman could be.

The elegance of the official quarters gave me the feeling I was about to face the King. His Majesty, Mr. M., sat behind a desk the size of Gibraltar. He was a small, thin man in a grey suit with a wrinkled shirt and plain dark tie. His mouth was buttoned tight, but his eyes had a shining quality and an open gaze. I had no defense against that rapier look. He saw everything, even that one glove and the subway grease on my new shoes. I knew *he* knew I had not driven up in a taxi.

Ordinary little woman, he was thinking, and scared.

In time, I grew to be very fond of him and to know he really was a great editor, and also to call him by his first name and not worry over how I looked, but that was a good many stories later.

He waved me to a chair, and if he spared a greeting I did not hear it. "About the ending of this story," he said. "I want you to change it."

I pressed my shaking knees together and looked at him, this little man who affected the destinies of so many writers as well as illustrators, assistant editors and staff. In moments of stress my throat closes, but I managed to produce a squeaky answer. I did not utter any deathless prose.

"Why?" I asked.

"It doesn't fit," he said. He made a dismissing gesture with one airy hand. "So if you will just do it over, we are prepared to buy it."

Now I heard my own voice with surprise. "I don't want to change that ending."

He shrugged, obviously thinking that here was another silly writer and how tiresome all writers were.

Of course I could change the ending of that story, just let him dictate what he wanted, type a page or so extra, and not only have my piece in the magazine but oh, how we needed the money!

But this was my story and my ending belonged in it.

I knew it was an editor's business to know more than the author, not only about the mechanics of a story or book but about reader sensibility, with which he—or she—has had far more experience. Further, he did not have the author's ego, which can be overwhelming and often ruins otherwise expert writers. But I had a deep inner feeling that these particular characters inevitably moved toward this particular ending— which now I cannot even remember, so it could not have been world-shaking! I expected to abide by editorial requests for most of my working life, provided I was lucky enough to be published.

I was also, I sensed, going to read hundreds of short stories and books and observe that some firm, considered editing would have made them better.

However, I summoned up every scrap of courage in me and looked at Mr. M.

"I think my ending is the way it would happen," I said.

He swiveled his great chair around and stared briefly out at the grey city.

"Suppose you explain it to me," he said. His voice was like shaved steel, I thought (and I must remember that to use sometime).

I knew my explanation was silly and would not affect the great man at all and that I was a stupid, bungling, be-

ginning writer with only a few published pieces. But I had
lived with the people in the story until their bone marrow was
my own. Oh, yes, they were mine. Even the thought of
what my family would say did not influence me in this
crisis.

Half an hour later I crept out of the office with my
manuscript still lying on the shining expanse of the desk.
It would come out, with my original ending, in the December
issue.

"Send me your next," he said.

The next story I wrote, I revised several times according to another editor's suggestions. I knew he was right and
that something had not worked out well. The beginning was
clumsy and not simple enough. There was a sag in the middle. Some of the dialogue did not ring true. It was a far better story with the editor's critical suggestions.

I learned a great deal about the craft of writing from my
experience with editors and felt sure I always would be learning. And I loved the discipline of a short story more and
more as time went on. In a novel or nonfiction book, one has
more scope, more time to spread out, so there is less tension,
but in a short story one word often must carry the weight of
several. The beginning, middle and end have restricted
shapes.

The short story, I decided, is really the sonnet of prose;
the book is like a long poem. I liked both but the form of
the short story was my first love.

Later, when I wrote a monthly column, I found being
a columnist also rewarding, for a column's brevity demands
a kind of economy of writing that makes it even more difficult than a short story. The complexity of life must be
distilled to make a column. When I went to museums to

look at great paintings, I usually liked the portraits better than the huge canvases, breathtaking as they were. I felt the artist put a whole life into one face in a portrait.

But being inconsistent, when I considered music, I preferred a great symphony to any short composition. A symphony affected me like the sea at full tide. Since nobody knew about my conclusions, I did not have to bother about being consistent.

Living in the midst of the Second World War could hold no happiness. Those of us who had been through the first one found the horror emphasized since we could not believe that this was the war to end war (we had heard that before). We just knew more about where battles were lost or won, for communication was better. Our grasp of geography was better, too. As the casualties mounted, they were not figures to us, for a man killed was part of us.

I myself hated war with a frightening passion which has never left me. Counting victory by bodies torn to shreds seemed utterly senseless. When our government reported light casualties on some front, I wondered at the dreadful impersonality of the men running the state. Ships were sunk, bombs fell on towns and peaceful countrysides, planes plummeted from the sky, and it all came down to adding up numbers like arithmetic.

When it was over, there was a kind of numbness for a time. We still woke at night listening for a roar in the sky, and all the homecoming parades seemed unreal. Our whole generation felt old and tired. Only the very young enjoyed the flag waving and the excitement of victory music.

But we went on making a living, raising our children, building houses or selling them, and in the end planning for the future (in which we hardly dared to believe). In the city the cocktail hour was popular and there were dinners with friends and nights at the theater, for money came more easily. There was laughter on the streets.

In small towns monuments went up in green cemeteries for the young who came back in boxes. Bronze plaques were put in public squares with names engraved on them and flowers blooming under them.

In time, our own young children would forget all about this war and have to study it in school in carefully edited textbooks. And the world governments went about their business of building more war material!

About this time I added a new experience to my working life. I became a regular monthly columnist for the *Ladies' Home Journal* and also wrote copy for a series it produced on remodeled kitchens. This was the heyday of magazines and even the splendor of the *Journal's* offices excited me. In the elegant kitchen-testing domain, fabulous dishes were concocted. In the dining room, parties were customary—complete with crystal, pure linen tablecloths, fine china. At one of these I met Eleanor Roosevelt. No picture of her ever did her justice, for the warmth and grace of her personality gave her a special kind of beauty. I met her again years later, and she held out her firm hand and said, "Gladys Taber, how nice to see you!"

Since I often cannot remember names, I was speechless. I longed to ask her how she could remember someone she met at a big luncheon—years ago!

My immediate boss was Alice Blinn, and she was the most gifted editor I ever met. I was so in awe of her that I kept swallowing my voice when I tried to say anything to her. I sometimes remind her of this today when we sit by the fire consuming crab salad sandwiches. Miss Blinn was a slim,

erect gentlewoman with carefully combed brown hair, keen
brown eyes and a resolute mouth. She usually wore suits in
different tones of brown and soft white blouses, with frills
at the wrists, reminiscent of Miss Mainwaring at Wellesley.
She did not have the slick, polished look of many women in
the field. Her manner was brusque, her speech direct.

In the beginning I felt awkward and very conscious of
the fact that nothing I wore matched. In fact, she scared me
to death. But I grew used to the way she picked up my manuscript from her orderly desk and said, "Sit down, Taber, I
want to go over this."

Her judgment was flawless, although penetrating enough
to make me ache at times. She never praised anything I
wrote, but before long I knew it was all right if she had not
blue-penciled more than a line or two. I began to count the
days until I could step again into that office and learn more
about my craft.

Some of the young assistants became good friends very
soon and when I came into the *Journal* enclave we hugged
and kissed and chatted. But Miss Blinn was a very private,
reserved person and we never even shook hands. In fact,
she referred rather scornfully to me as "the kissing Taber."
However, we did a lot of traveling on the *Journal* kitchen
series—to Michigan, Pennsylvania, Martha's Vineyard, New
Jersey, as well as all over Connecticut.

This was hard work and none of the staff seemed to
bother about eating so I was always hungry. One particular
day we had gone to Pennsylvania by car, and for some reason
the rest of the staff went back by car but Miss Blinn and I
took the train to New York.

"We'll go in the diner," said Miss Blinn, "and eat the
best they have got!"

We ate most of the way on that night trip, and one

of those miracles occurred for I suddenly knew we would be close friends the rest of our lives. We were not on official status, we were two tired women polishing off thick rare steaks and talking casually about ourselves. That was one train trip when I was too happy to be carsick!

The *Journal* kitchens involved a big staff that worked overtime, often under difficult situations. The basic plan was to choose all kinds of homes—mansions, old houses, apartments, cottages—to represent a cross section of America. The one thing they all had in common was a need to be renovated, remodeled, made better for family living.

There was, for instance, Alfred Lunt and Lynn Fontanne's New York city apartment, where I had the excitement of a bread-making session with Alfred Lunt. He was as good at rolling out dough in the kitchen as he was at delivering lines on the stage. There was a development house in Michigan which was not yet finished. It was one of Barry Wills's designs, built around a core. There was a Colonial mansion or two, an ancient country farmhouse, a suburban frame house in a block of the same type.

Once a kitchen was selected, the amiable, gentle photographer took pictures of the kitchen as it was. Miss Blinn and C. Eugene Stephenson, known as Steve, who was the designer-decorator, began to make plans and the home appliance members conferred. Mr. Luer, the *Journal* carpenter, was enlisted to build extra tables or shelves as needed.

There were also local electricians, carpenters, plumbers, painters as required. This meant that when things were under way it was like the middle of a football field in a tie game, both teams driving for that touchdown! I sat in a corner with my black notebook trying to write it all down, and sometimes after a few hours I had trouble making sentences.

Once, in a very difficult kitchen job, the local workmen all left at four thirty. Steve, who has had a bad back ever since, hauled furniture and climbed to the ceiling to hang drapes. By the time everyone was suffering battle fatigue, Steve was still cheerful, encouraging and hopeful!

Fortunately this job was in Mount Holly, New Jersey, so we made it back to New York by four o'clock in the morning. Steve was still unruffled as he said good morning and went off to his apartment in Greenwich Village to reassure his wife that all was well.

The greeting I got at home was, "Where have you been? I was just calling the police."

Steve and his charming wife were one more plus in my life, for a lasting friendship developed, and when they moved to the country they bought an old house on Jeremy Swamp Road, very near to the one we finally found.

Had I met Steve at a cocktail party, I would have felt he was the handsomest man in the world, with the grace and elegance of the true Virginia gentleman. But the Steve I grew to love was the man in shirt sleeves, a smear of paint on his curly mop, his trousers torn at the knees and his shoes white with plaster dust.

When this kitchen series was discontinued, I was happy to take the memories with me along with my cherished friendships. I suspect the deepest friendships come from sharing the hard as well as the easy times.

In this same period I did some radio appearances on the Mary Margaret McBride show and got a glimpse of another world. One disastrous day I substituted for Mary Marg when she was ill and only the deft management of Vincent Connolly, her emcee, made me able to cope, for on an ad-lib show there is never time to think or repeat. I acquired enough confidence to insert a plug for Sunbeam Bread, recommending it for cinnamon toast with tea by the open fire. Vincent turned pale but said nothing until the broadcast was over.

"We lost the Sunbeam account last week," he said. "Suppose the next time you leave the commercials to me!"

Not a good way to start a friendship, but we often remember that day now as we sit having lunch before an open fire. We settle for sandwiches on whatever kind of bread happens to be in the house! And I always tell him I ended my career with radio commercials on that one day.

My first television interview (I was the guest) was half an hour of misery. The hostess was one of those brittle ladies with brassy hair right from the shop, green eye makeup, orange lipstick and a dress that dazzled the eyes.

This occasion was supposed to be a friendly chat about my new book. Miss X greeted me with a condescending wave toward the chair. Then she dug around under the desk muttering to herself. It took five minutes or more for her to locate my book, which she swished through the air and dropped on the desk wrong side up.

I waited nervously to be interviewed, but I was well prepared on the material. It turned out Miss X had never seen the book before and had to whip it up to look at the title. She had obviously no idea what kind of writer I was or what the book was about. It is much easier to ask questions about any book if you at least know whether it is fiction or nonfiction. Under the circumstances I did not exactly sparkle, and when the miserable half hour was over, I fled.

But it was worth it, for it gave me a deep appreciation of interviewers who do read the book or at least find out who the author is. The interviewers who do their homework—Dick Cavett is one—are rarer than roses in a snow-drift.

With my book publisher I was supremely happy. For one thing, the whole atmosphere in that imposing domain was unlike that of any other place. From the receptionists to the secretaries to the two vice-presidents, I was made to feel at home. My natural timidity vanished the first day I went in. I had a curious and immediate sense that I belonged. I have never lost that feeling.

"You'll be happy with them," said my agent.

I never had that sinking feeling when I was asked to attend a conference or to go to lunch to talk something over. Instead of dragging in, I skipped.

Hugh Johnson, with an easy charm and great warmth of personality, would come in the office walking lightly and smiling as he laid down his pipe. He dressed elegantly but wore his clothes with a casual grace, as if he had just happened to pop into them. Most elegant, handsome men I have met have looked as if they were stepping in front of a camera for a color photograph as a VIP. He never tried to make his keen perception obvious. His quick sense of humor was never cruel. As time went on, I only found more happiness in knowing him.

George Stevens, the vice-president who was my editor until he retired and wrote his own masterly book on John Mason Brown, was the most brilliant editor I ever met, in fact an all-around genius. He did not fit into my preconceived idea of the Harvard man for he had a simplicity such as I never had known in so gifted a man. When we get together, I still am amazed that anybody can know so much about everything and have complete recall about anything ever written.

"Oh, that's King Lear, scene two, act three," he says gently.

But he is completely free of a trait common to some superintelligent men. He never takes over in a conversation in order to display his brilliance. He listens! Consequently, no one is uncomfortable with George. Sometimes, when general conversation grows tedious, I look at him sitting so quietly relaxed and smiling (a smile like spring sunshine in a garden). His blue eyes twinkle and I know he is thinking with humor about the peculiarities of human beings!

As an editor, he gave me complete security, for I knew if I wrote a single elegant sentence and impulsively repeated a figure of speech two hundred pages later, George would suggest that I had said that before. So I could write freely and as fast as my thoughts tumbled out.

"George will fix it," I said to the family.

We sometimes reminisce over the dinner table when he and his charming Laura come to visit, and we always come back to our only battle. It was about the spelling of the word "grey," which he suggested should be spelled "gray." I explained that *a* was the wrong color but *e* was a grey vowel and fitted, and I thought was reasonably correct, at least in early English.

"If you feel strongly about this," he said, "we shall spell it with an *e*."

His wife's only struggle has been to try to persuade him not to read while shaving, since he has scratches on his face as a result. We both agree we never knew another man who read while shaving!

When I wrote *Amber, a Very Personal Cat*, he turned me over to Tay Hohoff because he said he knew nothing about cats and she did. The result was my third great joy at being with my publisher. The two were poles apart in manner, but Tay was considered one of the great editors.

Unlike George, she never wasted time praising any part of a book. She was preoccupied with the mistakes, and I provided many since I am not a methodical writer. If anybody ever needed superior editing, I do. But after a book came out and we lunched at her favorite French restaurant, she would drop some offhand compliment over the soufflé. And she cared deeply about every book's being the best it could be considering the limitations of its author.

She was handsome, erect and with a purposeful walk (I had trouble keeping up with her). She had a clean, tailored look always. Her manner was brusque and she never indulged in trivia. Her voice was difficult to describe; the closest I can come is to compare it with an instrument in a symphony orchestra, possibly a trombone, rich and deep and cool.

I always made up my own titles until I wrote the book about Amber, my Abyssinian kitten. Titles were easy. But this I could not manage. Then I learned Tay had spoken up at an editorial meeting.

"Amber is a very personal cat," she said. And there was the title.

Our next problem was the cookbook. George said all he could do was fry an egg and this was for Tay to work out with me.

"Why not just call it *My Own Cookbook*," said Tay.

A cookbook is the most difficult kind of book for me since I always have hundreds of recipes but assume readers will know what a pinch of this or that is, and what size pan to cook a dish in. As to how many a recipe will serve, it depends on whether you are feeding six hungry people or eight dieters. The mechanics of this book took two years but Tay never gave up, although I often did!

My last conversation with her was about a country book.

"You have two thunderstorms in it," she said. "I think one is enough."

"They weren't exactly alike," I said.

"The first one is better. Can we cut out the second?"

"If you say so," I said.

"I love you, darling," she said and hung up.

It was left to Hugh Johnson to call me with the news when Tay died in the night, at home.

Then, during sleepless nights, I realized she knew all about her heart difficulty and in a roundabout way had tried to prepare me by talking so much about Peg Cameron, who might do my next book and whom I would be very happy with. Peg was, she said, a very gifted editor and a lovely person and exactly my kind, and she wanted me to meet her.

The relationship between author and editor is one of the most important. The editor must understand exactly what the writer is trying to do (effective or not). But also it involves a wide and wise view of the probable readership and what makes or breaks a book in terms of reaching the greatest number of those readers. It is, I think, one of the most complicated jobs.

I do not think authors can be their own editors, although some of them think they can. The author's perspective is limited by his own emotions and sensibilities. The driving need to communicate is in itself a limitation. The editor is the catalyst between author and public.

Perhaps if I had not been blessed with two great editors, I would have dumped my manuscripts in the old sea chest. As it was, I kept on letting the potatoes boil dry while I finished one more paragraph!

At that time, women's lib had not become a cause. It was no problem for either Jill or me; our husbands did not feel emasculated because we worked. The doctor was so proud of Jill for being the only lay member at that time in the Psychoanalytic Society, and Frank was grateful that I could help provide financially for our family. We were so fortunate to have no sex conflict. If I got held up on a job, he cheerfully ran the vacuum cleaner, took the cockers out for a walk and helped Connie with her homework until I got home.

But a working mother does take a toll of the children, for they are happier if Mother can be at home 150 percent of the time. This worried Jill and me and we spent a good deal of time talking about it when we did go to Central Park on a sunny afternoon or take our offspring to the circus (where we once lost Jill's son, David, for an agonizing hour). We also worried about the children spending all their growing years in the city.

"What we need is a place in the country for weekends," said Jill.

"If we could go Friday night and stay until Monday morning," I said. "All we need is a cabin or old barn and some land with brooks, woods, sweet meadows, wild strawberries. And free running for the cockers and my Siamese cat."

"Let's start looking next Saturday."

And that was the beginning of Stillmeadow.

Country Road, Lead Me Home

I HAVE WRITTEN thousands of words about Stillmeadow, the old farmhouse and its surrounding acres in Southbury, Connecticut. During the first years after we bought it, when Jill and I both lost our husbands after long illnesses, our weekends in the country kept us going through the long dark months. Later, when our children were away and we had no other regular responsibilities in the city, we combined households and moved to Stillmeadow for good.

I have written too about Still Cove, the house we built on Cape Cod overlooking Mill Pond quite a while after my cousin Rob Bagg and his wife, Bebe, had first introduced us to

Orleans. Both houses equally are home to me, though nowadays I find I spend more of each year at Still Cove.

But whether "home" means more the places—the quiet woodland and the flower-starred meadow in Connecticut, the blue-green water and the windy dunes of the Cape—or the people who have lived in the two houses and the neighboring villages, I cannot say. Sometimes "home" brings a flood of images to my mind, jewels from the unending cycle of seasons that are always the same, never the same. Sometimes the word makes me stop in wonder at the passage of time, the generations following one upon the other, the births and deaths that have altered my life beyond expression. I have written of many of these things too—of the living beings, both animal and human, who have blessed my existence. But there are always more that I remember afresh, or that came into my life only yesterday.

Not the least of the gifts Stillmeadow gave me was the opportunity to have an Irish—the first since Timmie. City life was well suited to cockers, but it would never have been possible to raise Stillmeadow Hollyberry Red in our apartment in New York.

Holly was bred to be a champion, and the time eventually came when she was expected to uphold the family tradition and get her championship in breed. Art Baines said he would handle her and that she was a natural. We had promised Paula, her breeder, that Holly would not be the only descendant of a long line of champions not to make her championship. So we would see it through. This was easy to promise when she was a handful snuggling up to me. But when the time came and I realized she must travel around with Art and be *away* from home nights, I found it almost impossible. Art was so patient that he worked out a plan whereby he would meet us at some crossroad, pick her up and meet us again after they came back from Detroit or Boston or wherever. Not only were we unable to make the round of shows with her, but Art said he would prefer us to stay away.

The first time we met him at some roadside bar and grill, I saw that his enormous car had a bevy of prospective champions in the back in screened carriers.

"She has never been shut up," I explained. "She always rides in the front seat."

"Well, it's time she learned," said Art, pleasantly, while Holly climbed all over him. The last I saw was the car driving off into the sunset and Holly's tail still wagging.

"I cannot go through with this," I told Jill.

"Well, let's try a little while," she said.

I now realize how patient Art was with me, for usually when a handler takes a dog for a championship he does not have to keep meeting the owner at odd hours so his charge can go home for a weekend or even for one night! I also suffered some damage to my ego for Holly loved Art and would always leap back in the carrier. Art said she loved showing; she knew she was a champion from the beginning.

A few times Art allowed us to go to a nearby show, provided we hid behind the hot-dog stands, so I could see Holly move into the ring, plume flying, muzzle lifted and pride flowing out of her. She made me think of the royal family of Britain riding in an open carriage, so secure in their sovereignty. But I felt in my own humble way that I should have a silver loving cup just for letting her go off with Art.

The trophies piled up until we had a long-distance call from Langley Field in Virginia and Art's easy voice said,

"Our girl made it today. You can meet me at that coffee shop about nine o'clock Tuesday."

"So what are you crying now for?" asked Jill. "She is a champion!"

"I'll never let her out of my sight again," I sobbed.

"We ought to put her in a field trial someday," Jill said.

When Holly was to get her tracking degree we took her ourselves since the trip was in Massachusetts. And in obedience classes we were always with her right through Utility Dog, the final degree. For the rest of her life, I never went anywhere that she could not go with me.

When she died of a stroke at sixteen I was thankful we had not missed any time together except for that championship period and at the same time I always knew Art was right, that she was born to show and deserved her career.

As I think of it, I do not know how I managed to get Holly to any of the right places at the right times when she was at the height of her career. Not, anyway, when I was following somebody's directions to a place I had never been. I find most people's instructions about roads and turnings and distances no better than my own. (Jill always told me I confused people by my travel advice, such as, Watch for a red barn on a hill, or, There's a side road here, don't take it; turn right at the Olde Kettle antique shop.)

I will never forget our first trip to visit Faith Baldwin. At that time it was supposed to take about two and a half hours to get there from Stillmeadow. (Now in this superhighway age, it takes little more than an hour.) Her map of instructions was a classic. We were hopelessly lost for some hours and saw more of lower Connecticut than we wanted to. We finally (terribly late for lunch) found the big white mansion. I was driving and managed to take down a very special shrub in the long, winding driveway. Then we got to the house and up the steps to the big front door. After banging on it with no result, we wrestled with it. It was nailed shut but it gave in as the nails came flying out. Faith was quite properly at the back door around the corner of the house.

After we went in and stopped apologizing, we had cooling drinks in the beautiful living room while the patient cook tried to reassemble lunch. Before we went into the dining room I visited the powder room to freshen up while Faith and Jill took a look at the garden. I had quite a stay in the powder room because I got locked in.

I felt sure no guests Faith ever had made such an impression. But it was only the first of many happy returns, although we got lost again on the way back, and it was dusk-dark before the cockers and Irish and cats swarmed over us, obviously having given us up forever.

So much has been written about Faith Baldwin, giving essential facts as to her fame, her books—over a hundred of them—her wide efforts in more important causes than can be counted, her brilliance as a public speaker, that her public life is thoroughly covered. Our viewpoint of her did not have anything to do with this; she was our best friend.

Our first impression was that she was so small to have done all she did. In the spacious big house she looked rather like a doll. But the moment she walked in a room, the air was electrified. We found out that in any group she is the focus with her dazzling wit, instant perception and interest in any subject. Her compassion for all people is a rare gift in this curious age.

The only way she had a trace of snobbishness was that she felt being unable to cook was somehow a limitation.

Once when she was with me and I was laid up with flu, she decided to get my breakfast. I had just fallen into a doze after a wretched night when I heard her tapping footsteps. She held a grapefruit in one hand, a carving knife in the other.

"Don't let me bother you," she said, "but how do I cut this?"

At that point I got up and rescued the burning toast in time.

However, athough she was raised in an era when gentlewomen never stepped foot in the kitchen but gave the list of guests to the butler, her relationship with her servant staff was far from traditional. They were her friends, her family, and she was always more concerned with making them happy than with what they did for her. Her warm friendship extended to every member of their families.

When she visited us in the old farmhouse, she adapted with easy grace. She insisted on lugging her own suitcase up the ladder stairs unless it was heavy as a steamer trunk. She borrowed a dust cloth to dust her bedroom. She made her own bed, and since she is not much larger than a pillowcase the results were hilarious. The heavy, handwoven bedspread was always her undoing and would cascade to the floor.

In our circle of friends Jill and I invariably chose the same favorites—Faith was certainly one of them—and that circle was always expanding to include more. When I remarked on how we always agreed about people, Jill said, "We both have good taste, that's all!"

Among our favorite friends were the Tomeys, who used to run the small meat market in Woodbury. They were young, beautiful, gentle and gay. They were Lebanese by heritage and they had a kind of dark elegance obviously not

Yankee. By the time they moved to Southbury and enlarged their business, we felt like relatives. Today the market in Southbury is a supermarket and although I cried when the new building went up, they understood for they, too, felt a sadness.

"We ourselves will not change," George Tomey told me.

George is a quiet man, reserved, almost shy. He has the only eyes I have ever seen that are the color of blue gentians. His brother Joe is outgoing, exuberant, full of laughter, and although there is a family resemblance, Joe's eyes are dark as midnight under dark hair. He is possessed of such a fine voice that at one time when Victor Borge lived in our village, Victor offered to set him up as a singer.

"I thought it over," said Joe, "but I couldn't leave Peggy and the children and travel around all the time."

He settled for singing in church and at village festivities, which may be one reason Peggy looks so happy.

Louis was the middle brother, who lacked the dark handsomeness of the others but had a special grace and sweetness so people lingered by the meat counter just to feel happy. When he died very young and very suddenly, the whole village was stricken. Even now after a number of years, when we gather at the supermarket, we all speak about how we miss him and how much he gave to our lives. We all feel he is still there behind the counter.

Beyond Woodbury, by a narrow road leading through deep woods, lived another friend we cherished. His name was Grey Fox and he was an authentic Indian Chief, descended from Colonial forebears. He ran a flourishing antique business, chiefly because he loved fine old pieces of pine or maple. We met him when we were hunting for a pine chest for the upstairs bedroom. He was not the Indian of the movies. He was a tall, erect man with skin a butternut color and close-cropped hair. He wore no Indian trappings but well-fitting grey-blue trousers and a spotless shirt open at the neck. He spoke better English than most of us and whatever he uttered had wit and wisdom.

He lived in an impeccably clean rustic cabin. We always felt humble when we visited him, remembering what our ancestors had done to his people. Jill and I were especially grateful that he gave us his friendship, for our road was once the old Kettletown Road leading to Kettletown, which was land the settlers bought from the Indians for a kettle!

The only remains of Kettletown were a small cemetery with a few leaning headstones marking the graves of Revolutionary soldiers, but we still felt apologetic as we sat on Grey Fox's porch talking about antiques. He was a private man and never referred to his ancestry or to the fact that the Indian tribes were defrauded of their rich lands in Connecticut.

Personality is a strange thing. Like my old Virginia friend, Colonel Murray Edwards, Grey Fox would share much with us except the past and often as we dropped in just to visit, we never asked him questions. We knew there was a wall we could not climb.

There were no walls, however, between us and the Lovdals. When we met them their farm was a storybook place. The white, rambling farmhouse is not quite as old as Stillmeadow but dates back to the 1700s. The barn in back of the house held the dairy herd unless the sleek black and white cows were grazing in green meadows. The barn is not like the huge midwestern ones we knew but smaller and more beautiful, with hand-hewn beams—the kind of barn that people nowadays are buying to remodel as homes. The inside was all white and so clean we wiped our feet on the wet grass before we went in the first time.

Oscar Lovdal used no milking machine, no conveyor belt to roll the feed along. We were introduced to every cow by name, with comments on the varied personalities.

That first visit took place in the late afternoon. Golden light shimmered through the windows. The air smelled sweet, with hay and grain in the feeding troughs, and was like the very essence of summer. Jill and I felt such a sense of peace there that we hated to leave. We stopped in the square addition to the barn where Oscar housed a steel tank for the milk, which was picked up daily by the milk truck. When he opened the top, the rich creamy milk was almost golden in the light. It seemed to me melted pearls would not be as pure.

Oscar is what they call a scientific farmer, with a degree in forestry from an agricultural college. But this does not really describe him, for he is what we call in our valley a born farmer, who works his land himself without a crew of farmhands and a ton of fancy machinery.

After the excitement of visiting the cows, we went to the house for one of Jean's marvelous dinners—barbecued spareribs, hot homemade bread, a salad savory with herbs, fresh fruit and creamy cheese for dessert.

Jean is an artist as well as a gourmet cook and yet farm woman enough to help cut five cords of wood, run the hay baler, help when calves are born. She also sings beautifully. Before train service was discontinued in Seymour, she went in to New York for the opera. She only gave that up when Brewster became the nearest station.

"It isn't fair to have Oscar make that trip at dawn and begin milking the minute we get back," Jean said firmly.

Their sons were in the Peace Corps for some time, and they are still living in native villages teaching the people how to grow crops and feed their families plenty of good, wholesome food. The color photographs the Lovdals have make one feel the steaming jungles are paradise! The youngest Lovdal is the daughter currently still in college.

When I sit with them in the living room after dinner, the room is filled with the glow of candles, which Jean says is prettier than electric light. We talk of books, music, politics and local affairs. We admire the rush-bottom chair Jean is working on and the antique table they have done over.

Both of them have their roots deep in Southbury, although their heritage is Scandinavian, and a few years ago, while a caretaker baby-sat with the cattle, they went back to Norway and Sweden to hunt up relatives. They even, they said, managed the language fairly well.

They make me feel inferior much of the time, not only because of their infinite skills but because of their sparkle and their ability to live completely every day as it comes. Oscar is quiet, Jean volatile. Both are slim and move with grace.

Long hours in the hayfields have turned Oscar's fair skin the color of early autumn leaves. His blue eyes are framed with crinkled lines from summer sun and his hair is a silvery gold. In his gentle, whimsical mouth there is invariably a slim-stemmed pipe which he rarely bothers to puff.

Jean's face is oval, finely boned, and the winds of her emotions ripple across it constantly. Her straight hair is brushed back and sometimes confined at the back of her neck. In any case, it never falls over her grey-blue eyes.

My favorite memory of her is when Amber, my Abyssinian kitten, had to have an emergency operation. Of course it was midwinter and the roads were like skating rinks. Jean turned up early in the morning to drive us to New Haven (Amber and I were alone). Dr. Whitney promised to do the operation immediately. Meanwhile we had more sleet, snow and ice.

I knew the roads were impassable but Jean turned up anyway in their rather battered car. She said it was no problem and off we went. While we waited for Amber, Jean opened a box on the seat of the car.

"Imagine you haven't eaten anything," she said.

There was hot black coffee and warm spicy gingerbread in the box. I ate a whole square and drank the coffee and felt restored.

When we got home, Amber, swathed in thick bandages, refused to lie down but staggered around on two legs and a half. Jean built up the fire, fixed a hot toddy and sat with me the rest of the day. She was my personal rescue squad and I have always told her she saved an extra life.

The next day she brought a chicken casserole with wine sauce. "Just in case you don't feel like cooking," she said.

The farms in our countryside are vanishing. Oscar says people cannot afford to farm in New England anymore. Several years ago the Lovdals sold all but thirty of their cows. Jean watched them being loaded in the trucks and cried. We thought of what it meant to have no more of that rich, creamy milk going daily to New Haven. Perhaps in another generation children will survive on powdered milk or some new synthetic product but I cannot believe it will be the same.

One thing I have always loved about our Connecticut village is that it has room for all types of people. Two immediately come to mind, one whose name I do not even know, and another whose name should be carved on a monument, though he is still very much alive, thank heaven! The first was so insular as to be a total mystery, while the other in a way has involved himself with our entire continent.

The first was a hermit. On our way to the village we sometimes stopped at the small shack where he lived. Like a traditional hermit, he was a mystery. He was very thin and wiry. He had dark hair and very dark eyes. But unlike the storybook hermit, he was clean-shaven and had a look of cleanliness about his khaki pants and sweatshirt.

The shack was homemade, built out of bits and pieces, with only a narrow stovepipe poking through the roof. A nameless dog idled around, always friendly. A small garden patch was behind the shack but there was no henhouse.

When we stopped, our hermit was courteous and friendly but shy. He sold luscious ripe strawberries and sweet honey but there was no sign announcing this to passersby. He could not possibly have made any money with his casual sales and we always wondered how he survived.

My efforts to find out something about him, even his name, would have done credit to Lord Peter Wimsey but were less successful. A few rumors circulated. The one I liked best was that he was a college man and did have money somewhere but "something had happened." No one really ever knew, and it did not matter. He was perfectly safe there in his small insulated world.

George Bennett, our first mailman, was the other. He came only as far as the corner mailbox, but if there were packages too large for the box he drove on down to our house and blew his horn. There was, and still is, no such thing as Special Delivery in our village, but often Miss Evangeline telephoned from the post office to tell us there was something urgent.

George Bennett is one of those rare men who truly have become a legend in his own time. He is now known as "Mr. Conservation" and has many awards for his work, last year even going to Washington. He has dedicated his life to conserving the natural resources and wildlife in our valley and his pleasant, white farmhouse is visited by people from all over the country who wish to help.

He is a typical Yankee, if there is a typical anyone—spare, erect, weathered, keen-eyed, slow-speaking but with a generous smile. The fact that he has one wooden leg with a square peg at the bottom has never deterred him from climbing hills, hiking along riverbanks to study erosion, planting trees and shrubs in inaccessible places.

He changed our lives, casually and forever, the first day he drove to the gate with a load of big packages in the front seat. The backseat was full of seedlings and various bushes.

"Now you people have moved here," he said. "I see you changed your address."

He unloaded the mail, leaned against the picket gate and said to Jill, "See you started a vegetable garden. This is good land, was a good farm once long ago. I notice that slope above the swamp needs some planting."

Frankly, we had been limiting our efforts to the small area around the house.

"Oh, my!" I said, weakly.

"I just happen to have some willow seedlings in the car," he continued. "The lower edge of your pond would be good for them and help keep the pond from flooding."

The next thing we knew we belonged to the farm bureau and a conservation organization, and when George blew his horn, Jill said, "I know, we have to plant something!"

One of the most important friendships we ever had began that first day. Before long we were frequent visitors at his house where his rosy, apple-cheeked wife taught us all we needed to know about canning, preserving, or raising house-plants as we sat around the big table consuming chicken fricassee with feather-light dumplings and oh, what gravy, followed by apple pie.

My passion for African violets was shared by Ethel Bennett, and I often dropped in when one of mine was ailing and tried not to be envious of her houseful of violently healthy ones blooming their heads off.

I always remember one Sunday afternoon when we crawled up a steep hillside, grubbing out rocks and planting bushes along a road some distance from our land. We had planned, for once, to take the day off after church and rest our aching bones. But George phoned to say he had a load of things that needed to be put in and could we meet him?

We met him.

I doubt whether he would appreciate a statue in the center of town to memorialize what he has accomplished. He would only say, "Pomperaug is polluted and the bank's eroding. Let's take care of it."

Jill was an avid learner. Often as I was trying to finish a book or a column, she would poke her head in my bedroom door and start to talk.

"George says—" she would begin.

It might be what to do about the Japanese beetles in the rosebushes, or how to graft a tree, or whether we could trans-plant any of the lady's slippers from the upper orchard, or what fish to stock the pond with, or the best variety of sweet corn for our soil, or what to do about oyster scale on the lilacs.

In fact, any problem that came up was resolved simply. "I'll ask George," Jill said.

He seemed to know everything about nature. His knowledge was encyclopedic and it came not from any degrees but from his own experience.

And when I reflect on what George Bennett has accomplished, I realize one man with a dream can affect more lives than we could imagine and do more to preserve our heritage. It is easy to say I cannot do anything to contribute to the country because I am just an unimportant citizen. But one rural mail carrier in one small village never bothered with such thoughts. His memory will be forever green and his influence will never cease.

George could help us by advising what to plant at Stillmeadow and how and why to plant it, what to clear away and what to preserve, and we depended heavily on him for this kind of expertise. But we could not expect him to solve all the other questions that had to do with keeping things going. At least some of those questions were financial, and Jill and I often found ourselves in a hopeless tangle when it came to taxpaying time.

Our problem with managing finances ended in a way that made us believe in miracles. Joe Cassidy came into our lives when everything seemed more complicated than any crossword puzzle. Jill was very good with figures and kept elegant ledgers, whereas I could not even add or subtract and have a gift for losing receipts. But even for Jill the income taxes were a nightmare.

Joe is a big, easy man with a smile that reminds me of Irish music. He is the kind of man who folds his handkerchief exactly right in the upper pocket of his elegant suit. He is a careful man who wears rubbers when it rains and takes them off before coming in the house. But he comes in snowstorms, 90-degree heat or hurricane alerts.

Once in, he unpacks his briefcase and hooks up his electric calculator, or whatever it is, all the while telling a few hilariously funny stories. Tension evaporates and all those forms seem inconsequential. With the harvest table covered with files and folders, he and Jill used to sit sipping coffee as they coped. It was hard, tiresome work but I would hear them laughing now and then.

Somehow we even made our wills without feeling we would die the next week. I think many women and quite a few men put off making wills because it is too strong a reminder of the mortality of man. But I have seen too much tragedy resulting from this not to know how important it is.

We came to depend on Joe's frequent remark, "Don't worry, I'll take care of it."

When Jill died and Joe sat by the fire with me, I said hopelessly, "Joe, what will you do now you have inherited me?"

"Don't worry, I'll take care of things," he said.

I cannot help feeling there is something wrong with our society when an average person cannot cope easily with taxes, insurance, property values, balancing medical expenses and so on. As one of my dearest friends says, "I wish I had a Joe Cassidy. I suppose he wouldn't move to New Jersey?"

It is easy for me to be dependent but Jill was strong as granite. Still, it was not long before Jill would say, "I think we should put copper cables on all the giant maples. We seem to be a lightning nest and they practically overhang the house. I'll give Joe a ring and see what he thinks."

One special gift he has is complete recall. It used to take Jill hours to ferret out some past expense but she gave that up.

"You paid such-and-such a sum five years ago in June," Joe said. "I think it's time to get that job done again. Better have the chimney cleaned out, too."

I have never understood how one brain can hold so much but he does not find it unusual at all. Furthermore, his idea of relaxation is to play championship bridge or teach his grandson how to play chess, both of which require great concentration. He tells me he used to fish when he was a boy in Woodbury but doesn't fish nowadays.

The truth is figures are as exciting to him as poetry is to me. One day he called me in to say happily, "Gladys, there are *four* nines in this one balance! That wouldn't happen once in years and years!"

We were always in awe of Joe's ability but we viewed him as a specialist until his charming wife, Dottie, became ill and was in the hospital for a very long time.

"How can you manage?" I asked.

"Oh, I do my own cooking," Joe said. "I clean house and do the laundry and get to the hospital twice daily. But I don't need a lot of sleep so I can start my own work sometimes around four in the morning."

Then he added with that lovely smile, "I am a pretty good cook but the neighbors ask me out a lot for dinner."

It seems to me that the George Bennetts and the Joe Cassidys in the world (though I doubt there are really any others like them) know exactly who they are and what they are capable of. Perhaps this comes with growing, for I never knew them when they were boys. I wonder if at one time they were as unsure of themselves as my young friend Erwin.

Erwin came to be part of Stillmeadow as Tommy's replacement. Tommy was my neighbor George's (another George!) grandson, who came after school to do odd jobs just as his father, Willie, had done before him. When the time came for Tommy to go full-time to the technical school, he brought Erwin around.

"You can use him instead," he said.

Erwin was so shy he held his head down as he mumbled hello. Nobody could be less like the exuberant, volatile Tommy than this small boy, peering with difficulty through misfitted glasses.

Willie always felt Stillmeadow was his real home, Tommy knew he could run it better than we could, but Erwin stood mute, waiting to be told to take out the trash.

When finally one day he strode in saying firmly in his light, hesitant voice, "I am going to take the trash out first and then clean the fireplace and then I think I'll rake the front yard," I went in my room and nearly cried, I was so happy.

My life with Erwin had all the excitement of seeing a tight bud open into a full blossom. So I began to look down the country road again, waiting to see the small figure, wrapped in woolen scarves in winter, trudge from the bus to the gate. He always looked so small and vulnerable against the background of giant maples and the swamp.

Part of the pattern repeated itself, since he also went to Danbury to the technical school and worked at a supermarket besides. But he never missed a day with me. By the time he was fourteen he could turn the car around in my small driveway after a trip to the village so that I could get out without falling into the pond.

He also was the one who could help me give Amber whatever the doctor prescribed. He held her wrapped in a bath towel while I swabbed her mouth with a horrible cherry kind of liquid for gingivitis and we mopped his sweatshirt afterward.

He was a complete nonspeller so we played Scrabble daily and kept a list on the bulletin board of new words he learned. The list would have staggered any English teacher, for it ran from gingivitis to ecology, but we had fun with it. One time I especially remember was when we drove to the village to shop and I was explaining about the color in the sunset sky. He had his license by then and was busy making the turns on Jeremy Swamp Road. In the midst of my enthusiastic discussion of shades of color, he gave me a sidelong glance and slowed down.

"You know what you are?" he asked. "You are an eccentric."

"Oh, Erwin, how wonderful you know that word! Yes, I am," I said.

For me, this was a moment that was forever.

I was alone during the worst winter storm in a hundred years, with snow brimming the windowsills, the wind sounding like a wolf pack, and the last log falling to embers in the great fireplace. Around midnight I looked out and saw a flickering light on the road. There was Erwin, up to his neck in snow. He managed to shovel the back door open.

"Just thought I better come and see if you needed more wood for the fire," he said calmly. He admitted he could not get his car down that road, so he had walked.

We had many experiences, including his first trip to a bank to open a savings account. He was scared to go in but I shoved him. The teller was a friend of mine and welcomed him warmly, and when Erwin put his first earned money on the counter he suddenly grew in stature.

Now he is a highly paid IBM electronic worker. I wonder if he ever remembers that first day at the bank!

Erwin had, I found out immediately, two opposing characteristics. He put himself down, as Willie said. He was incredibly insecure. But he never gave in to defeat in any circumstances. He would keep at anything, from rehanging a storm door that did not fit to fixing my new typewriter after I had given up. Most of the instructions for the type-writer were in German, which is his family's native language and my favorite next to Latin. He made out some of the words and studied the pictures with grim concentration. None of the words were part of my academic German vo-cabulary, and the illustrations made me dizzy.

Erwin worked into the night, and when I tried to stop him he gave me his wide, gentle smile.

"You need it," he said.

When I praised him extravagantly, he wiped his square palms on a piece of tissue. "I didn't really do anything," he said.

"You gave me my typewriter, darling."

"Shouldn't have taken me so long. I'm just dumb."

I am happy to hope IBM appreciates him, and since they raised his salary three times before he had been there very long, I think they do. But his characteristic remark never will change. "I'm not really worth it."

Sometimes I feel like Mrs. Chips, I have watched so many boys grow. Almost as soon as we began going to the Cape, Bobby Gibson brought special happiness to us there by turning up at the door to see if we wanted the lawn mowed. The lawn consisted of a patch of weeds with a few spears of grass, but I would have had Bobby mow the sand itself. He was ten years old, thin, fair-haired, sensitive, utterly appealing. Like our David, he had asthma, which made us feel he belonged at our house. As he grew, he began to take over any chores we had and became a part of our lives as if he were our own.

After he was through with school Bobby began to work with a carpenter, for his dream was to be a builder, to create houses. We often talked about this. We would bring pizzas from the nearest pizza place and have them for supper and spend the evening playing our favorite folk music.

"I want to build houses," he said, "as soon as I have learned enough."

Last year he built a house for Henry Morgan, the television personality.

"Did you have any trouble getting your home built?" Henry was asked on a TV interview.

"I have a Cape Codder for my builder," Henry said, "and everything went fine. He is a very gentle man."

I have seldom known anyone pursuing his chosen career so steadily. By the time he was established as a contractor, Bobby was able to build a home for his bride, and now his small son follows him around learning how to hammer and saw and make things.

My current boy, David Gilmore, graduated from the Cape Cod Community College and now works at the old-fashioned country store, Ellis's, which is such a treasure to those of us who do not like the huge supermarkets. David is built like a football player, although hockey is the game he plays regularly. When he steps in a room the furniture seems diminished. Under a cap of seal-dark hair, his dark eyes shine with his zest for life. His dream is to be a photographer and his photographs are so good they often appear in the newspapers. He has a special gift for action shots at sport contests but he also has a creative view of nature, which results in beautiful views of the Cape.

"The blue heron is on your beach," David will say. "I'll just run down and try for a shot."

Grabbing his camera, he races down the steps, slowing

as he nears the shingle. He is always looking for something good to take a picture of.

I know how lucky I am that I can count so many young people as my friends. They give me a feeling of continuity and companionship which I might otherwise miss. For inevitably, as the seasons passed at Stillmeadow and Still Cove, our lives changed. The children outgrew summer camps and went off to college. They built separate lives and those were difficult times, as they are for all parents. Surely it was only yesterday that Barbara and Connie had their secret hiding place in the woods and left notes for each other in a hole in the trunk of one of the last old apple trees. It was yesterday when David rode all day on our neighbor's hay truck and suffered the worst attack of asthma of his life. Wasn't it last week when we bought the farm and had a feast with a huge steak cooked in the open fireplace embers?

Death did not forget us. When my mother died, I was alone with Father. I remember how good and gentle the nuns at St. Mary's were. The chapel in the hospital was on the same corridor as Mama's room and the nuns always found time to kneel there and pray for me and for her.

Father and I got no comfort from each other at that time. Father once more broke his relationship with God, as he had when Majel and Walter died. He resented me for being alive and he blamed the doctors and nurses for Mama's dying. I am wiser now than then and would understand, but I accepted the fact we were strangers as we stood on opposite sides of the bed, both of us losing the mainspring of our lives. We rarely spoke. Sometimes we met in the long, dim corridor, Father striding furiously and I walking bent over and with dragging feet. It was the time we needed each other desperately but were unable to communicate.

My alienation from him was complete over a childish reaction to the fact that my mother's most exquisite piece of jewelry, a diamond, platinum and jet brooch, was pinned on her silken bosom in the coffin but Father took it off before the coffin was closed.

I have come to believe that when a mother dies there is a special reversion to birth with her child. The newborn baby leaves the security of the womb and undergoes a dreadful battle to emerge into a difficult world where he must breathe for himself with the lifeline cord to the mother severed. When the mother dies, the process is in some way repeated as the source of his being vanishes. Scientists may not agree with me, but this was my experience.

Father came back to a normal world although he never felt the same deep love for me again, and in time he remarried happily. And he went back to church.

Our life-style changed after Jill and I lost our husbands and the children went away to school. Belle went back to Nameless, Virginia, to live with her daughter, and the big apartment was given up. Jill stayed in my small apartment while she still worked in Harlem, and for quite some time I went back and forth between city and country.

We picked up the fragments of our lives and tried to maintain a family unit, and it was the children that made it imperative. They, too, had been through the deaths and disruption of families.

Sometimes Jill would say, "Suppose we had never bought Stillmeadow—what would have happened?"

"We would have no home base," I would say. "We would have just drifted."

Journey to Tomorrow

DOWN BY THE POND at Stillmeadow the air is sweet with
spring. The spillway sings with tumbling water on the way to
my neighbor George's brook, and the willows are golden
fountains above it. Jill planted those willows years ago, slim
saplings. Now they seem to touch the tender blue sky. The
slope rising from the pond to the wood is gold, too, with the
daffodils she put in. In May the wild violets bloom there so
thickly one must walk on them to climb the hill.

The small screened house we built on the ancient stone
foundation of an early cabin is damp, for the hand-hewn rock
wears beads of moisture. The smell of stone and moist timbers

is rich and cool. The dark water of the pond sends a breath
of sweetness, too.

I like to sit on the bench and listen to the sound of
silence and dream my individual dreams. If I turn my head,
I can see the world of reality, for the sturdy old farmhouse
is there and the giant sugar maples surrounding her. The
lilacs can now look in the attic windows and the well house
is smothered with wisteria. How much of my heart belongs
to this place!

When I go back, I can hear the voices of the grandchildren as they come in from the upper meadow. It is a light,
lilting sound filled with the melody of youth. It belongs to
spring itself.

When I indulge in reverie I can imagine that the voices
are Connie's, Barbara's and David's. But it is Alice, now
fifteen, and Anne, now thirteen, who ride their bicycles down
past Jeremy Swamp.

Ellen, Jill's oldest granddaughter, has just graduated
from Yale with Phi Beta Kappa tucked in the record, and
Davy, the grandson, is making his mark at Haverford. He has
Jill's ability as a photographer and his photographs have the
rare quality of a creative artist.

Big David, Jill's son, with Anne, his brilliant wife, three
children and practically a zoo of animals, lives in Princeton.
David is a psychiatrist and is also on the Rutgers faculty.
Anne is now doing research at Rutgers. David says it involves
her spending her time with rats. Jamie, Betsy and Amy are
still too young to choose careers.

I can go back in time in about one minute and remember when Barbara married Val, who has brought so much
into our lives with the grace of his personality, his calm,
balanced wisdom and warmth of heart. Barbara's successful
career in Cornell University's extension department in New

York and Val's position as vice-president of the Amalgamated Garment Workers Union have not interfered with their life as parents and homemakers.

Connie now teaches English Literature at Barnard and Curtis is working overtime in the exciting new field of film documentaries, which gives our family group about as much diversity as one could imagine. When they all get together, the old farmhouse vibrates.

I have a favorite memory of Curt. He came in my room one day not too long after the wedding at Stillmeadow. He stood in the doorway, tall, slim (he can eat four helpings and never gain an ounce), and his sensitive face simply glowed.

"I just want to say, Gladys," he said, "I was so afraid of having a mother-in-law! Now that it turned out to be you, everything is fine."

I am glad that the grandchildren all had a chance to know Jill before she died. My memories of that period are too personal to be told, but I can recall how understanding the children were during the time I was dazed with grief. They never even said the wrong thing, which I imagine is something of a record.

When the children left, our old friends Erma and Joe Vanek drove down the road every day to see how things were going. Also our young minister found time to drop in very often, not to preach or quote the Bible but just to visit. Sometimes I asked him before he left to give me a prayer. I wish I had been well enough to write down those prayers, for they were as refreshing as a cold spring in a desert. But I never wrote down anything until I had set my feet on the new path I was to travel, and then I wrote *Another Path* to gather my feelings.

Now as I walk up that path from the pond, I feel a kinship with all the people who lived in the steep-roofed house. The early ones had a backbreaking struggle for survival, I know, clearing boulders and scrub from the land, planting crops with no modern tools, no tractors or trucks. A good many women must have wept as they bent over the washtub in the back kitchen, for children so often died young and adults had no benefit of scientific medicine as we have today.

A good many men must have walked the fields stooped with grief because their young wives died in childbirth. The patent-medicine man was not much help.

Then there was the period when parents had to arrange, or at least approve of, marriages. How much heartbreak was endured by young lovers! Many farewells must have been said in the old apple orchard at a secret rendezvous!

The very young were not immune. The small boys worked on the farm whether they wanted to go on to school or not. Too much book reading was a sign of weakness. Girls learned the household arts, such as spinning and weaving, cooking, embroidering and the proper way to put down corned beef. Even if they came from an affluent family (unlikely at Stillmeadow), a Female Academy or Ladies Seminary were the only educational goals, and these provided some French, some music (young ladies could play the piano to impress prospective husbands) and much training in manners.

The old Bullett Hill schoolhouse still stands in Southbury, and in time the children at Stillmeadow probably went to it. It is a one-room school so children of all ages attended. The modern school in Southbury is not far away in distance but light-years in time.

Now when I get inside the house, Curt is broiling a steak while Connie mixes the green salad. Alice and Anne stop playing their violins long enough to set the table. I can imagine what the long-ago families would say if Father ever went to the kitchen to prepare a meal. Curt is an excellent cook and spends a good deal of time in the kitchen. Also the idea of a fifteen-year-old and a thirteen-year-old seriously playing violins would be amazing. As for Connie, she can sit by the open fire after supper and read history, poetry or philosophy while I may spend a little time finishing a chapter on my own next book. Neither of us can weave or embroider or make clothes, although we wish some of the early arts and skills could have been taught us in our own childhood.

However, as I reflect on our time I feel sure the basic values of life are not changed, or the basic experiences. We are born, we grow into maturity, we die according to the law of nature. Our highly mechanized civilization has not redesigned the human heart. We find happiness, we suffer sorrow, we make our contribution to the world around us, whether it be a blessing or a disaster. Every man's life is entangled with others.

At Orleans on the Cape not long ago, my friend Olive and I drove to the old cemetery where a few early graves still stand in what is now a pine woods. A stone wall of glacial boulders protects it. Some of the oldest tombstones are bedded with soft moss but a few have legible carving. Most of them date to the early 1800s.

Many of the early folk died so young—thirty-two was not unusual and, for children, five. While I sat in the car, I could see Olive's tall figure pushing into the farthest thickets as she visited the past. My thoughts went further than any past known to man for the pale lemon light fell on that stone wall, the soft grey and faint pink of the wall a kind of monument to the incredible majesty of the glacial age. This, too, I thought, is our heritage, these indestructible boulders suggest eternity.

I felt peace sifting down the sunset sky and with it a faith that those whose names were carved so long ago were not gone. I sensed their presence, my heart listened to them. Such a mystic moment is not to be forgotten.

Olive is a quiet person, but as she got back in the car she said thoughtfully, "I liked walking in those pines!"

That particular journey to yesterday ended when we got home, where Olive's lively miniature schnauzer and my own airborne Abyssinian were impatiently waiting for fillet of fresh flounder. Olive's Siamese was at her house in deference to Amber's feeling that she must be the only cat in her piece of the planet.

This being a day of reverie for me, I began to think about jealousy. In human beings, I am told, it indicates insecurity but I have seldom lived with a more secure being than Amber. Does her small head contain a fear that another cat might seem more wonderful to me? My friend the skunk, Blackberry, does not bother her a bit. Nor does the schnauzer. But two raccoons in the yard once sent her screaming through a crack in the door in a jet plane attack.

Jealousy in humans is usually no more reasonable than Amber's. I have known it to destroy more relationships than almost any other trait. Pride may go before a fall, but jealousy goes before destruction. We do expect small children to be troubled by it as they walk with unsteady steps into the vast world, but most manage to outgrow it if parents are careful.

My era has seen an upsurge of another destroyer which we now label Archie Bunkerism. It flourishes in wartime and our three wars have been fertile ground for it. But hating anyone of another race has a colossal stupidity about it I cannot endure. Discriminating against those of another color is just as destructive.

If our country were inhabited only by white Gentile descendants of John Adams, say, or Robert E. Lee, it would indeed be flat, stale, unprofitable. The ethnic groups which immigrated gave us a rich and varied society that bigots never sense. And, after all, as I sometimes point out to racists, there was no choice for you as to your place in society, you acquired no merit except that you were born. Why should you feel so superior? What matters is what you do with the gift of life.

True greatness lies in loving your fellowman. It only involves seeing every human being as an individual, which is what we ourselves expect.

I myself do not like to be classified as I often am: "Oh, well, she's a writer." This implies being eccentric (I admit I am), lacking in sound sense, a little flighty and perhaps just plain peculiar. No two writers are alike except they must work at their job—just as millions of others do!

However, in our society a great many men and women cannot choose their jobs or careers. We all know of some who spend half their lives at work they do not even like, only to discover too late they would have been fulfilled in some other field. I hope someday children very early will be encouraged to develop in the direction they most desire and be helped along the way.

There really is no limit to the types of occupations in this country which, despite its defects, is the closest to a classless society on earth. We are not born into a caste system. And nowadays women have a chance to work in fields that were formerly closed to them. I admit I am still old-fashioned enough to think men do some things better than women and women do others better than men! But recently I heard several women coal miners declare they had no difficulties! As one who is always scared of being in a subway, I cannot imagine how they feel, but I am sure my way of life would appall them.

A few special people find scope for their talents in very unexpected places. My friend Jimmie DeLory, who runs the service station in Orleans, has been an unofficial counselor for dozens of boys who have held summer jobs with him.

His wife Eileen combines bits of driftwood and a few seashells to make works of art.

And then there is Vicky Smith, gentle, shy and self-effacing, who is a gym teacher in a New Jersey high school and teaches her students courage and determination as well as tennis and basketball.

The last time I was at still Still Cove I dipped, in imagination, into a profession I once knew nothing about. Two very dear friends came to see me early one evening. Dr. Howard Gotlieb is an archivist for the Mugar Memorial Library at Boston University. His profession involves tracing important documents and memorabilia to be preserved for future generations. A priceless record of our time is being gathered in this wonderful library. Some of the correspondence of famous men and women is to be locked in vaults for fifty years before being made available to scholars and students and the public; some may now be studied. This is an arduous task indeed, for everything must be authenticated and catalogued. Dr. Gotlieb's encyclopedic knowledge is combined, however, with an easy wit and a warm, friendly charm. He looks at the world through dark, laughing eyes as if life were amusing, but when he speaks of the troubles his investigations uncover, his gentle voice is compassionate and understanding.

Bill Adams, who came with him, is an architect who has the rare quality of being able to listen. He has the quietness of a cool woodland spring. When he is pushed for a comment on some controversial issue, he says something that is really important. He sits smiling, relaxed, absorbed in his thoughts. But without arguing, he can impress the rest of the group with his inner depth.

After this visit, my young friend Linda dropped in to report that all the shelves in the kitchen in the bank where she works had suddenly crashed to the floor, along with a full set of dishes, pots and pans kept there for fixing snacks and lunches. Linda is the head teller at one of the Orleans banks and also works at night for Kim Schneider, our beloved veterinarian. Linda combines a passion for banking with a love for animals almost equal to mine. I always feel as if I jumped from the bank to the examining room at Kim's in half a minute as she recounts the happenings. Linda looks like one of those improbable *Vogue* covers. She is so tall she bends her head when she comes in the door. With her slim, long-legged figure she reminds me of a filly at the starting gate in a Derby kind of race. But when she talks about either of her jobs, she is suddenly mature.

Just as Linda got up to leave Barbara and Slim Lovely arrived. They had been taking a moonlight walk on the beach and Barbara brought me a nosegay of sea lavender. It had to go on the top bookshelf where Amber could not reach it—she has a passion for it and it always makes her sick. The Lovelys seldom leave the Cape, yet their interests are wide-ranging and our conversation moved from politics to books to gardening

It was an evening for visitors. Slim had just put another

log on the fire when Millie and Ed Connors turned up, on their way home from supper in Wellfleet. For years they have been the mainstay of my life at Cape Cod. Ed comes over to put up my hurricane shutters before I even hear that a storm is expected and Millie knows before I do when I need to buy more coffee or defrost the refrigerator or get a new raincoat. Tonight they were full of stories about their new black kitten. He would never, they said, be allowed to sit on the dinner table as Amber always did. Of course, it would be all right if he perched on the shelf just above the table. . . .

Friendship means sharing interests and this means widening one's horizon. It involves loving kindness and patience, never faultfinding or criticism. Too often I hear people explaining just what their friends have done wrong. I do not consider this true friendship!

Am I perhaps impatient with faultfinding people because my own dearest friends seem neither to have faults themselves nor to find them in others? They seem always to be giving generously of themselves, without question or pause, and even the smallest of incidents will remind me of this.

For example, there are my nearest neighbors, Kay and Pret, who live in a house next to mine on Mill Pond. I remember a short time ago when I was trying to start my car and it made a lot of noise but would not move an inch. Before I could get out, Pret came rushing down the road.

"Sounds as if you are having trouble," Pret said.

I made my appointment on time!

Pret is a champion fisherman and I may come home from town to find a bagful of freshly dug clams or some flounder fillets while Kay pops in with a bouquet of their elegant garden flowers or some new peas and fresh lettuce. Being a good neighbor is an art which makes life richer.

One person I love to visit is Helen Beals, on Rock Harbor Road. Helen has six grandchildren so the big white mansion is often bouncing with youngsters. Helen has the rare ability to manage even if they come for a weekend without notice. Sometimes when she does expect them, they do not come and I admit she is better natured than I would be if left with a couple of gallons of milk and a big roast of lamb! Her generous nature, however, is only one of her assets. She has a delightful sense of humor and a wide range of interests, and conversation with her is always exciting.

Summertime explodes on Cape Cod and at Stillmeadow. Seasons in New England never gentle into one another. I always believe summer will never end until one morning I see the first swamp maple glowing scarlet. The excitement of autumn leaves me breathless, for it is hard to absorb the splendor. It is as if a painter swept every color on his palette at once.

Comes the brisk morning when the first gold leaves ride the air to the country road, and surely this is accidental! But the snowflakes drifting from a November sky write winter's signature. Those first flakes circle as they fall and Amber runs from window to window trying to catch them. They seem like cool white stars dropped from the pale sky.

Winter brings a quiet time for growing things to rest. The mystery of nature is most evident to me as seeds sleep beneath the full tide of snow and sap is quiescent in the maples. Now we know the snow itself nourishes the earth, bringing nitrogen. Only the evergreens seem unchanged, except the green is darker. Or is it because of the white world around?

On Cape Cod the landscape is deep with them, for this

is evergreen country. The scrub oaks let no leaf fall, so the
copper-red makes a brightness along the roads to the sea.
The sea herself is a green-blue, sometimes silvered along the
beaches with ice. The sky seems wider somehow. It is patterned with the wings of the sea gulls.

For us human beings, winter should bring a thinking
time, a re-evaluation of our lives. On bitter January nights we
sit by the open fire and watch the shifting colors in the embers. There is time for good conversation, for reading books
laid aside during the busy summer. There is time for music
and for memories.

December brings Christmas, which is a time for families
to be together as we celebrate the birth of that small baby
who was to be more powerful than any king or emperor or
dictator. This man of peace and love still moves our hearts
although temporal rulers are long forgotten!

The Christmas tree itself is a symbol of immortality
with bright green tip reaching toward the sky. The glittering
ornaments make the house bright and holly and mistletoe
add their rich color. The spicy smell of pine blends with the
perfume of bayberry candles and popcorn exploding into
snowy sweetness in the ancient wire popper. If we are lucky
we may have chestnuts roasting on the fire shovel.

When I was small, the tree was garlanded with popcorn
and rosy cranberries, strung patiently on fine string. We had
a spun-glass star for the tip of the tree. Now we have a gilt
star and there are boxes of ornaments collected over the years.
If one is missing, the grandchildren hunt feverishly until
they find it. They, too, build their memories!

There has been a tendency of late to commercialize the
holiday season but the real spirit of Christmas cannot be lost.
I remember the year Jill and I decided to forego the tradi-

tional plum pudding and hard sauce flaming with brandy (which always flickered out at once). The children had never liked plum pudding. But that year they spoke as one. "Where's the plum pudding? We always have plum pudding."

One minor change did take place. I used to read Dickens's *Christmas Carol* on Christmas Eve while Connie and David and Barbara toasted marshmallows. They all knew it by heart as Jill and I certainly did, but it was tradition. Later, when the grandchildren came along, there seemed to be no room for it in their Christmas Eve.

I think the modern tempo does not encourage reading aloud and it is a pity, for it was a family sharing. It must go back to when books were so few and houses were not flooded with light. After supper, families settled down while Father read aloud by the one good light in the living room, a big oil lamp with well-trimmed wick and later an Aladdin lamp which cast a white glow on the table.

The reading-aloud habit persisted through most of my childhood, although we did have electricity. Father liked to read aloud, as I do, and he had a beautiful musical voice. Mama would sit quietly and sew while I held my Irish on my lap (or as much as was feasible). Mama's gold thimble shone as her small hands flashed up and down over lace or linen. Occasionally Father read Greek—and why did he never teach it to me?

A good many men and women who broadcast, I have noticed, do not really read their scripts well. They read word by word, thus losing the rhythm or the impact of a sentence. I wonder whether it dates from the time when reading aloud went out of the classrooms and the home?

In the early days at Stillmeadow we spent a good deal

of time protecting the tree ornaments and gaily wrapped packages from kittens and puppies. My Siamese, Esmé, especially loved the glass icicles. The puppies dashed about, trailing clouds of tissue and scarlet ribbon. Neighbors dropping in waded through the debris.

Late on Christmas night the house quieted down and I had time, as I still do, to step out by the old well house and look at the eternal sky and think about the people all over the world. God rest you merry, gentlemen, is my greeting.

The New Year in our valley is usually the beginning of the long cold. It is the time of the Full Wolf Moon. The sound of the snow plow is its music. Since the energy crisis, the country houses seldom string red, green and blue electric lights on the evergreens in the yards but most have lamps or bright candles in the windows, which is a warmly welcoming sight. Some home folk decorate an outside Christmas tree with food for the birds and the happy flash of wings is a special beauty!

New Year's means neighbors dropping in for eggnog and bringing homemade jams, jellies, fruitcake or elegant cookies. We sit and talk while the last log glows on the hearth.

We never went to Times Square when we were in New York, or to any big-time famous eating places. To me there is a kind of desperation in the massing of human beings at this season, as if they all were frightened because a year has gone.

My celebration begins in the morning with a small Abyssinian cat jumping up and down on top of me to suggest she is hungry. The gentle sounds of the old house herself are sweet and I imagine the ghosts of long ago have come to greet me and wish me well. If the sun is shining, it casts lilac shadows under the great maples and the snow is patterned with tracks from our wildlife friends. Chickadees, nuthatches, bluejays fill the yard with wings.

The voices of the children come from the kitchen where Curt is making pancakes to have with pale gold maple syrup. Connie is putting out pans of food for the barn cats who sit waiting by the well house. They come from George's barn but usually bring a few extras from down the road.

As the day goes on, snow melts on the wide floors, mittens and woolen scarves drape the radiators so the whole house smells of wet wool. The children tramp in the woods and, if the snow is not too deep, go to the bobcat's den to leave a New Year's gift of kitchen leftovers. Our woods and swamps and meadows have been protected for wildlife ever since Jill and I first bought the land. Occasionally hunters do get in, but Willie keeps a watchful eye out and last season chased a group of them away with his own old gun.

"'If you set foot on her land again,' he said, 'you'll never get off!" They ran, stumbling.

Willie is a powerful man, and when his temper explodes he really needs no gun! He can also move like a lightning flash, although normally he has the deliberate, slightly stooped tread of the true farmer.

Our best New Year's Day dinners were ham baked in the old wood stove in the early days but now we settle for the electric oven, which really does a good, if less romantic, job, and I admit feeding a wood stove is a constant occupation! I like real country hams studded with cloves and topped with pineapple circles and basted with their juice.

Some of Willie's big, mealy potatoes bake in time for dinner and we also like baked acorn squash with butter, seasoned salt and pepper and a dollop of that maple syrup bubbling in the cut halves. For dessert, chilled fresh fruit is our choice.

If we have a January blizzard, we stay by the fire and listen to records, read, talk—and we are a very verbal family so there is plenty of talk. Jigsaw puzzles are always at hand, as well as the latest crossword ones.

"Don't you ever get bored in the country in winter?" a city friend asked me.

My feeling is that boredom comes from within and has nothing to do with place or circumstances. There is always something to experience if we have the perception to sense it.

So as a new year begins, I take out my memories and sort them, the rough-cut jewels of my life. I relive them all and then put them away in my special box, laying the dark ones on the bottom and covering them over with the shining ones.

For now I have new experiences coming, new sorrows, perhaps, but new joys also. I have fresh opportunities to help someone who needs it, more love and understanding to give, and a renewed faith in God.

My journey to tomorrow is always just beginning.